Reforming the
Church Today

Reforming the Church Today

Keeping Hope Alive

Hans Küng

Translated by Peter Heinegg
with Francis McDonagh, John Maxwell,
Edward Quinn, and Arlene Swidler

T. & T. CLARK
EDINBURGH

1992

The Crossroad Publishing Company
370 Lexington Avenue, New York, NY 10017

Originally published under the title *Die Hoffnung bewahren: Schriften zur Reform der Kirche*, copyright © 1990 Benziger Verlag AG Zurich
This edition copyright © 1990 by Hans Küng

Printed in the United States of America
Typesetting output: TEXSource, Houston

Library of Congress Cataloging-in-Publication Data

Küng, Hans, 1928–
    [Selections. English. 1990]
    Reforming the church today / Hans Küng ; translated by Peter Heinegg with Francis McDonagh ... [et al.].
        p   cm.
    Includes bibliographical references.
    ISBN 0-8245-1045-3; 0-8245-1155-7 (pbk.)
    1. Church. 2. Church renewal—Catholic Church. 3. Catholic Church—Doctrines. 4. Catholic Church—History—1965– I. Title.
BX1746.K845213 1990
282'.09'045—dc20   90-38590
                                                                  CIP

Contents

Introduction: Keeping Hope Alive   1

Part One
STAYING IN THE CHURCH

1 Why I Am Staying in the Church   7

2 Why I Remain a Catholic   13

3 Catholics and Protestants: An Ecumenical Inventory   21

Part Two
OVERCOMING POLARIZATION

4 Parties in the Church?   31

5 For a Church of Renovation and Innovation   42

6 Church from Above — Church from Below   52

7 Longing for John XXIV: In Memory of Pope John XXIII   64

Part Three
SOLVING PROBLEMS

8 On the Way to a New Church Order: A Theological Case
  for Shared Decision-Making by the Laity   75

9 Free Election of Bishops: A Concrete Model   95

10 Women in Church and Society   101

11 Discussion on the Future of Pastoral Care   106

*Pastoral Care on the Brink of Collapse:
An Open Letter to a Pastor 106*

Collapse or Awakening? Bishop Moser's Answer 115

A Pastor for a Responsible Community: Reply 122

12 Worship Today — Why?   130

**Part Four
BETTING ON THE FUTURE**

13 On Fidelity   149

14 A Vision of a Future Church   155

**Part Five
EPILOGUE**

15 My Personal *Spero* — The Vision of a Better Future   169

**Part Six
DOCUMENTATION**

16 Declaration "For the Freedom of Theology" (1968)   177

17 Declaration "Against Resignation" (1972)   181

18 The Cologne Declaration: "Against Disenfranchism:
For an Open Catholicity" (1989)   187

19 A Call for Renewal in the Catholic Church (1990)   192

Sources   197

Introduction:
Keeping Hope Alive

I am convinced that the world's problems are much more depressing than the Church's problems, that the world ecumene is more important than the church ecumene, world peace much more urgent than peace between the churches. And yet I immediately add: How should the Church's suggestions for solving the world's major problems be convincing, if the solutions of the Church's major problems are bracketed out? How should the Church's commitment to the world community be credible if the community of the churches and religions is not drawn into it? How should the struggle of the churches for world peace be honest and effective, if the lack of peace between the churches continues to remain a cause of so many tensions and divisions among peoples?

Precisely at a time when everywhere in the world a deep longing for peace has broken through, where in a power system like the East bloc a fully unexpected awareness of political freedom, human rights, democracy, and pluralism has dawned, and a general renewal is on the way, in the age, that is, of *perestroika*, *glasnost*, and *solidarnocz*, the Church should proceed with its own internal reforms, which had such a hopeful beginning in the Second Vatican Council (1962–1965).

To be sure, we reform-minded Catholic theologians find that nowadays, quite differently from the conciliar period, the official Church sometimes blows a harsh wind in our faces. But is that a reason to slacken in commitment to church reform? Is that a reason to give up work for the Church? No, this is just the hour to keep hope alive, the hope that reform of the Church in head and members can and must go on. This is why I decided to publish this book. It is aimed at sending a signal to the disappointed and the resigned: There is reason to keep hope alive.

Perhaps the reader of these various pieces will be able to sense how strange it felt for me to reread everything that I had written on the subject of church reform over the last two decades. On the one hand I could not quite repress a feeling of melancholy. How much has been

1

demanded for decades now — and has not yet been realized. How much of what was written long ago sounds brand new. How many demands, requests, wishes of countless Catholics, which I have taken up in my talks and essays, have been rejected or simply ignored by the official Church.

On the other hand I am overjoyed by the realization that my own work for church reform in the light of the present, hopelessly backward-looking course is perhaps better understood now than in earlier years. Innumerable Catholics have become aware that current Vatican policy is on a wrong course, and the captain is on the point of steering the ship into dangerous waters. Ten years ago I had the feeling that I was almost alone in my criticism of the present pontificate (and alone in having to pay a price for this). Nowadays disappointment over the current course is something everyone is talking about. The "Cologne Declaration" by 162 Catholic professors of theology from German-speaking countries, which I add as documentation for this book, is only the tip of the iceberg. It stands in historical continuity with earlier declarations by theologians who likewise expressed their concern about the throttling of the spirit of reform in our Church.

These two epochal declarations of 1968 and 1972 — documents of Catholic theology's self-respect — have also been included in this book for the sake of historical continuity. Throughout the book it is important to me that readers recognize the problems addressed not as "my issues," but as "their issues," as their problems, which they are struggling with just as much as I am, and which I have voiced here only as their representative. The book aims to give a voice to those who have no voice in this Church.

And yet without the urging of my publisher I would not have republished these articles. But they convinced me that the right time for publishing this sort of book has come. Needless to say the various pieces are different in form and importance. Many are dependent on the immediate situation to which they were addressed. And yet in the course of editing the book (in which my co-workers Eleonore Henn and Margarita Krause, along with my colleagues Karl-Josef Kuschel and Stephan Schlensog, provided help for which I am grateful), I myself was surprised that there was very little overlapping between the individual articles, so that the editorial adaptations could essentially be limited to occasional changes of titles. It also became clear that between these individual and disparate contributions lies a consistent overall concept of the Church, where both the grand lines can continually crisscross and the individual details can mesh.

I have already presented this basic concept of the Church in my book

2

The Church (1976), and these brief essays cannot be understood without that fundamental theological book. But I hope that even someone who doesn't have that large volume in hand will sense in reading this one that three features shape my ecclesiological thinking:

1. *Christian radicality:* All statements on church reform are not based on adaptation to a *Zeitgeist* or sociological and practical considerations, but on the key document of Christianity. All demands for reform have their "radix" here. They are furthermore supported by the great Catholic tradition and formulated with an eye to the needs and hopes of people today.

2. *Constancy:* Without wavering and hesitation, without opportunism, without concessions to the Church's "court theology," I present here a concept that has integrated the basic impulses of the Second Vatican Council, and that has been systematically thought through for two decades and made concrete with an eye on practice. None of the demands for reform is derived from a purely inner-church enthusiasm; rather they are formulated realistically and constructively in view of what is now already possible within the Church.

3. *Coherence:* The individual demands for reform do not stand alone and isolated but are a part of a consistent general conception. Questions such as celibacy, the ordination of women, and the laity's share in decision-making are not casual questions of detail, but an expression of an internally coherent notion of the Church. This concept is centered on the gospel. It concretizes the transformation, introduced by Vatican II, of the Catholic Church's total constellation (paradigm change) — away from the Middle Ages, Counter-Reformation, and antimodernism — in the direction of postmodernity.

One more point. Essays I have written that directly criticize the current course by the Vatican were not included here. They can be read in *Katholische Kirche — wohin?* (Whither the Catholic Church?) edited by Hans Küng and Norbert Greinacher (Munich, 1986).

I dedicate this book to my oldest theological friend, Wilhelm Klein, who celebrated his hundredth birthday this year, his mind alert as ever. For my part, this is not just a sign of gratitude for everything that I have learned in theology and spirituality, and experienced in fidelity, from this tremendous man. It is also a sign of continuity in my life. The ideas expressed in this book were given their foundation in my student years in Rome (1948–1955). My basic motives, my intellectual commitment to the Church have not changed since 1954 when I was ordained a priest of this Church in Rome. Of course at the time when I was thinking of practical pastoral work and not something like a university career, I could not imagine how the prayer on my ordination holy card, phrased after Col. 4:3, would be fulfilled: "Pray for me that God may give me an opening for preaching, to tell the secret of Christ."

This book was put together in the tenth year since the revocation of my permission to teach as a representative of the Catholic Church. I feel that this is a particularly important sign. The attempt to silence a critical voice failed. On the contrary this book shows my determination — in season, out of season — to continue my way for this Church in hope.

Not the least thing I learned from Wilhelm Klein was that we can trust the spirit of God, which is the spirit of Jesus Christ, but that we can also go on working, struggling, and praying for a renewed Church in the service of a renewed human race. I learned that we can do this with the staying power of hope in patience and calm, but at the same time with imagination and energy, without any arrogant claim of always being right, but without any anxiety, either, as we work for an ecumene of the Christian churches, preparing the way for the ecumene of the world religions and the ecumene of the whole human family.

Part One —

Staying in the Church

1 —

Why I Am Staying
in the Church

Is leaving the active ministry a signal for leaving the Church altogether? The prediction was made some years ago, but now even those who refused at that time to believe it have to admit the fact: the Catholic Church is threatened by a massive exodus of priests from the active ministry.

Petitions to Rome for laicization are climbing into the thousands, especially from the United States, Holland, and the Latin countries, and above all from priests in religious orders. In 1963, there were 167 who left. In 1970, the number was 3,800! And there are in addition the many who do not bother to ask permission. It is estimated that in the last eight years some 22,000 to 25,000 priests have left, 80 percent of them ranging in age from thirty to forty-five.

Even more threatening for the future of the Church, though, is the rapid decline in ordinations, a decline of some 20 to 50 percent, depending on the region. (In Germany the number of young men entering the seminary has dropped 42 percent in the last eight years, and sometimes only a third of those who enter are actually ordained.) If things continue in this way, many a seminary will be able to close its doors. Then, at least, some bishops and Roman authorities will open their eyes. On December 22, 1970, Pope Paul told the College of Cardinals how much he was distressed by the statistics of priests and religious leaving; but he did not announce any decisive measures to counteract their departures.

There are various reasons why priests are leaving the active ministry. The law of celibacy is one of the chief of these. It is being maintained — with every possible means of moral coercion — against the will of the majority of those concerned. The question here is one not only of "professional interest" but even more of fundamental human rights. At issue is the welfare of our communities and that Christian freedom which, on this very point, is anchored explicitly in the gospel. It is precisely with respect to the question of celibacy that the coercive measures of a still largely preconciliar, authoritarian church system become glaringly visible to everyone, and especially oppressive for priests. According to the latest surveys, 40 percent of the young Catholic priests in the United States (but only 12 percent of the Protestant clergy) are giving thought to leaving the ministry. The chief cause: a lack of leadership from those in authority and the slow tempo of change after Vatican II.

In such a state of affairs, a priest may well ask himself: why not me too? This is especially so when, in addition, he receives considerable mail urging him to leave. Some of it comes from people outside the Church: they think it is a waste of time and energy to remain in a rigid ecclesiastical system when more could be accomplished outside it. Other letters come from people inside: they think that radical criticism of conditions and officials in the Church is not consistent with staying in it.

Now it is clear that leaving the active ministry does not necessarily mean leaving the Church. The fact that so many priests are giving up their ministry does mean, however, that the very people who are most involved in the Church are dissatisfied with it. Their leaving the ministry has become the alarm signal, therefore, for a withdrawal at various levels from the Church, the signal for a widespread emigration — interior and sometimes exterior as well — out of the Church. Along with religious indifference, the chief reason for leaving the Church is repeated annoyance with its system — clericalism, confessional narrow-mindedness, the laws regarding mixed marriage, birth control, and divorce. Under these circumstances, one hears that even bishops find it difficult to answer convincingly the question of why they are staying in the Church or ministry. Hell no longer poses a threat for one who leaves. Secularization of modern life and awareness has removed many social pressures for staying. And the age of cultural Christianity seems to have come to an end.

But can a question such as this be answered briefly at all? A book on the Church is a more adequate response. But if the question is posed, then a concise, direct answer is called for, an answer that is personal as well, since obviously the question involves more than theology.

One important reason why many Christians stay in the Church — perhaps up to now the reason for most of them — is the same reason why people stay Jews or Muslims: people are born into a particular community; whether they like it or not, they are formed by it and remain affected by it, either favorably or unfavorably.

It is no little thing for us to remain on intimate terms with our family or to leave it in anger or indifference. For many, at least today, this is still a reason for staying in the Church and also the active ministry. They wish to struggle against the rigid ecclesiastical traditions that make being a Christian so difficult, even impossible. But they do not wish to give up being a part of the Church's great Christian tradition that goes back two thousand years. These Christians wish to submit Church institutions and constitutions to criticism, whenever people's happiness is sacrificed to them. But they do not wish to give up that which is necessary in the way of Church institutions and constitutions. Even a community of faith could not last long without these, and all too many people would be left alone precisely in their most personal problems. These Christians wish to resist Church authorities when they presume to lead the Church with their own ideas instead of with the gospel. But they do not wish to give up the moral authority which the Church can have anytime in society when it acts truly like the Church of Christ.

Why am I staying in the Church? Because, in critical loyalty, there is so much in this community and its history that I can affirm, so much in this community from which, like so many others, I draw life. I am staying in the Church because, along with the other members of this community of faith, we are the Church. (One should not confuse the Church with its apparatus or administrators; nor leave it to them alone to mold the community.) I am staying in the Church because, with all the strong objections against it, here I am at home. Here all the great questions are asked: the where and whence, the why and how of human beings and our world. I could not think of turning my back on the Church any more than, in the political sphere, I could turn my back on democracy, which, in its own way no less than the Church, is being misused and abused.

Of course, there is also the other possibility. And I have good friends who have chosen it. In the light of its decline, some have broken with the Church for the sake of higher values, maybe even for the sake of being more genuinely Christian. There are individual Christians outside the institutional Church, perhaps, in short-lived boundary-situations, groups of Christians as well. I respect such a decision and even understand it. During the present depression in the Catholic Church — following upon the conciliar euphoria under John XXIII — I understand more than ever why people leave.

I could certainly give as many reasons for leaving as those who have left. Jumping ship for some may be an act of honesty, courage, protest, necessity, or simply the inability to take any more. For me personally, though, it would be an act of weakness, failure, capitulation. I helped sail it in better days; should I give up the ship in a storm? Should I leave

9

it to others, with whom I have sailed, to stem the wind, to bail out the water, even to struggle ultimately for survival? I have received too much from this community of faith to be able to leave so easily. I have been too involved in Church reform and renewal to be willing to disappoint those who have been involved with me. To those opposed to renewal, I do not want to give the pleasure of my leaving; to the partisans of renewal, I do not want to give the pain.

Every day, every hour, the work of Jesus is in truth being accomplished by the witness of ordinary Christians who are making the Church present in the world. And so this would be my decisive answer: I am staying in the Church because I have been convinced by Jesus Christ and all that he stands for, and because the Church-community, despite all its failures, pleads the cause of Jesus Christ and must continue to do so.

Like other Christians, I did not receive my Christianity from books, not even from the Bible. I received my Christianity from this community of faith, which has managed to make it through these last two thousand years; which, time and again, one way or another, has managed to call forth faith in Jesus Christ and involvement in his spirit. This call of the Church is far from ringing true as the undiluted Word of God. It is a very human call, all too human. Despite the many false tones and distorted actions, though, the message can still be heard. Its opponents point out with justice how often the Church has been in discord with the biblical message it preaches, how often the Church has been a tyrant, a Grand Inquisitor, or a shopkeeper, rather than the representative of the work of Jesus Christ. And yet the message has been heard.

Neither do I wish to give up the greater effectiveness that is possible in the Church. The other alternatives — working in another church or outside a church — do not convince me. Schism leads only to the isolation of individuals or else to new institutionalizing, as the history of ecstatic religious movements has shown.

I cannot take seriously the Christianity of an elite who pretend to be better than everybody else; nor church-utopias which imagine ideal communities made out of ideal people. Is it not more exciting, interesting, challenging, and, ultimately, also more satisfying and productive to struggle *in* this concrete Church of human beings for a "Christianity with a human face"? Here at least I know who the opposition is; here there is a constant challenge — to responsibility, to active involvement, to stubborn endurance, to vigilant freedom, to resistance in loyalty.

And now, when the authority, unity, and credibility of this Church have been so deeply shaken because of the evident failure of its leaders, now when the Church shows itself all the more as weak, wandering, and searching for direction, now — rather than in times of triumph — it is easier for me to say: I love this Church — for what it is and for what it could be. I love this Church, not as a mother but as a family of faith. It is for the sake of this family that the institutions, constitutions, and authorities exist at all. Sometimes one simply has to put up with them. Where it truly functions as a community of faith, even today, despite all its terrible defects, it is able not only to inflict wounds but also to perform wonders. This community still can and does perform wonders wherever it not only serves as the place for remembering Jesus (although that alone is something), but also in word and action truly *pleads the cause of Jesus Christ*. Quietly, without publicity, through people in the pew rather than through bishops and theologians, this community, with all its faults, is doing the work of Jesus.

Whenever the Church truly pleads the cause of Jesus Christ, whenever it carries out his work, then it stands in service to humankind and becomes credible. Then the Church becomes a place where individual and social needs can be met at a deeper level than today's consumer society can achieve. Here, with faith in the life of the One who was crucified, that reality can be accomplished which uprooted individuals and a shattered society so desperately need: a radical new humanity, where law and power are not abolished but rather relativized for the welfare of humankind; where guilt is not reckoned up, but endless forgiveness can be found; a humanity where positions are not simply maintained, but unconditional reconciliation is accomplished; a humanity where the higher justice of love replaces ceaseless squabbles over rights; a humanity where merciless struggles for power are replaced by the peace that passes all understanding. No opium, therefore, which gives hope only in the hereafter. But rather a summons to change the here and now, to change society radically by changing the individuals within it.

Whenever the Church, more rightly than wrongly, pleads the cause of Jesus Christ in its preaching and active assistance, it brings together rich and poor, men and women, high and low, black and white, the educated and the uneducated, uniting them in the solidarity of love. Whenever the Church heads the cause of Jesus Christ, it makes initiative and action possible on behalf of freedom and peace in today's world. And perseverance in the struggle for freedom and peace is made possible, even where there is no prospect of success, where neither social evolution nor the socialistic revolution can overcome the tensions and contradictions of human existence and society. Pointing to the cross of the living Christ — the distinctive characteristic of Christianity — the Church makes it possible for people not to despair of justice, freedom, and peace, even in the midst of unfathomable injustice, slavery, and war. The faith of the Church makes it possible to hope not only when times are hopeful but also when they are hopeless. It makes possible a love that embraces even enemies. It makes it possible for people and society to be humane even when people spread nothing but inhumanity.

No "Hymn to the Church" should be sung here. But it should be pointed out what faith in the crucified Christ, preached by the Church, can accomplish. For this does not all fall from heaven; it does not happen by accident. It is mutually related and affected by what takes place in the Church, its preaching and worship, modestly enough, but maybe today again in greater freedom. It happens when a pastor preaches this Jesus, when a catechist teaches Christianity, when an individual, a family, or a community prays from the heart without empty words. It is brought about when baptism binds a person to Christ, when the Eucharist is celebrated with implications for the community in its everyday life, when a person's guilt is forgiven out of the power of God. It is made possible where service is given to God and human beings; where the gospel is truly preached and lived through instruction and involvement, dialogue and pastoral care; in short, whenever Jesus is followed and his work taken seriously. In this way the Church can help humankind. And who should do so *ex professo* if not the Church? It can help people to become and to remain more human, more Christian, more Christ-like. In the light and power of Jesus, it can help people to live and to act, to suffer and to die in a truly human way in the world today, because they are thoroughly supported by God and are committed to their fellow human beings unto the very end.

It depends on the Church how it gets through the present crisis. Its program is a good one. Why am I staying in the Church? Because I draw *hope* out of faith that, as in the past, the program, the cause of Jesus himself is stronger than all the misconduct in the Church. In spite of everything, for the sake of the cause of Christ, it is worthwhile to be involved in the Church as well as in the active ministry. I am not staying in the Church *even though* I am a Christian. I do not consider myself more Christian than the Church. On the contrary, I am staying in the Church *because* I am a Christian.

Why I Remain a Catholic

On December 18, 1979, the Sacred Congregation for the Doctrine of the Faith issued a "Declaration on Some Major Points in the Theological Doctrine of Professor Hans Küng." The declaration accused Professor Küng of having departed in his writings from "the integral truth of the Catholic faith" and pronounced that "he can no longer be considered a Catholic theologian nor function as such in a teaching role." In particular, Küng was charged with "contempt for the magisterium of the Church" on the issue (among others) of papal infallibility, as expressed most recently in Kirche — gehalten in der Wahrheit? (The Church — Maintained in Truth). *What follows is Professor Küng's response.*

Why do I remain a Catholic?

This is not an easy question to answer in the midst of a time- and energy-consuming controversy, when it becomes almost unbearable to write at all. After an unjust and unfair procedure on the part of the highest ecclesiastical authorities, I was deprived by decree of the title of "Catholic theologian" and an attempt was made to drive me out of my faculty of Catholic theology after twenty years of teaching there and to thrust me — without being overscrupulous about methods — to the margin of my Catholic Church very shortly after I had completed twenty-five years as a priest and celebrated my jubilee. In the face of harassments and threats, is it possible to offer declarations of loyalty or to make professions of faith?

Under these circumstances, why do I remain a Catholic? From thousands of letters, telegrams, telephone messages, the same depressing question faces me, raised in sadness, anger, and despair in a variety of ways by innumerable Catholics throughout the world. Many are wondering if the wheel of history is to be turned back in our Catholic Church to the time before John XXIII and the Second Vatican Council. Are the new openmindedness, readiness for dialogue, humanist and Christian spirit again to yield to the triumphalism disavowed by the Council? Are Roman authorities again to abolish the freedom of theology, to intimidate critical theologians, and to be allowed to discipline them by the use of spiritual power? Are bishops to be merely recipients of orders and to be obliged to enforce the Roman policy on those who are under their care? And, despite fine ecumenical words and gestures, is the ecclesiastical institution with its unecumenical attitudes and deeds to become once more an unfriendly, inhospitable, unfruitful "fortress" in this modern society of ours?

This latest development has in fact already driven some to formal secession from the Church and very many more to definite internal emigration. This indeed is the most disastrous feature of the present ecclesiastical policy: the silent mass withdrawal from the Church will continue. And particularly those who as pastors, curates, and teachers have to dole out what the hierarchs have cooked up for them — that is, those who are looking helplessly for arguments to make the Roman measures intelligible in response to people's crucial questions — will want to know the answer to the question "Why remain a Catholic?"

A Personal Question

It is not any liking for theoretical problems which makes me raise this question, but the necessity of defense. For the doubts about catholicity are not mine; they are raised by certain authorities and hierarchs. Why then do I remain a Catholic? For me as for many others the answer must be first of all that I will not allow anyone to deprive me of what has been valuable and dear to me throughout my life. I was born into this Catholic Church: baptized, it is true, into the much larger community of all those who believe in Jesus Christ — nevertheless, born at the same time into a Catholic family which is dear to me, a Swiss Catholic parish to which I am always glad to return: in a word, into a Catholic homeland which I do not want to lose, which I do not want to abandon. All this I feel precisely as a theologian.

At a very early stage, I became acquainted also with Rome and the papacy, and — despite all calumnies — I do not cherish any "anti-Roman feeling." How often am I to continue saying and writing that I am not against the papacy nor am I against the present pope, but that I have always contended inside and outside the Church for a Petrine ministry — purged however of absolutist features — on biblical foundations! I have continually spoken out for a genuine pastoral primacy in the sense of spiritual responsibility, internal leadership, and active concern for the welfare of the Church as a whole: a primacy which might then become a universally respected authority for mediation and conciliation in the whole ecumenical world. It would of course be a primacy not of dominion but of unselfish service, exercised in responsibility before the Lord of the Church and lived in unpretentious brotherliness. It would be a primacy, not in the spirit of a Roman imperialism with religious trimmings, such as I came to know quite closely under Pius XII during my seven years of study in Rome, but a primacy in the spirit of Jesus Christ, as it was illustrated for me in the figures of Gregory the Great and John XXIII (as a theologian at Vatican II, I was able to observe him at close quarters). These were popes who expected not servile submissiveness, uncritical devotion, sentimental idolization, but loyal collaboration, constructive criticism, and constant prayer on their behalf: collaborators in our joy, not masters of our faith, to adopt a saying of the Apostle Paul.

At a very early stage, too, I came to know the Catholic Church as embracing the whole world and in it I was able to receive and learn an immense amount from innumerable people — many of them friends — everywhere. From that time onward, I have become more clearly aware that the Catholic Church must not become confused simply with the Catholic hierarchy, still less with the Roman bureaucracy.

But above all there was Tübingen, Protestant Tübingen with its Catholic faculty. Here as professor from 1960 onward, I have increasingly become a part of this faculty which, from its foundation, has had a great history, not only of success, but also of conflict. How many Catholic theologians in Tübingen, including some who are still alive and teaching, have been admonished, put on the Index, harassed, and disciplined! There is nothing new under the Tübingen sun.

It was from this Catholic faculty of Tübingen, in the free air of Tübingen, that both my books and the books of my colleagues emerged and without which they would scarcely have been possible or at any rate only in another form. In continual discussion with colleagues and students it was possible for a Catholic theology to emerge here, which — unlike the former controversial theology — has a truly ecumenical character and seeks to combine two things: loyalty to the Catholic heritage and openness to Christendom — in fact, to the ecumenical world as a whole. Discussion, particularly with Protestant colleagues, was of decisive importance, not in order to disparage the Catholic reality, still less to squander it, but in an ecumenical spirit to throw new light on it from the gospel and to gain a deeper understanding of it. Seeing this task as my duty, I was able in 1963 to switch over in the Catholic theological faculty

15

to the recently established chair for dogmatic and ecumenical theology. This position was combined with the direction of an Institute of Ecumenical Research which worked systematically for the convergence of divergent theologies without attempting to avoid questions hitherto regarded as taboo. Under these conditions, can a theologian be blamed for defending himself with all legitimate means against the pressure to get him out of this faculty of his?

Why then do I remain a Catholic?

Not merely because of my Catholic *origins* but also because of this *life task* of mine which is grasped as a great opportunity and which as a Catholic theologian I can fulfill appropriately only in the context of the Tübingen faculty of Catholic theology. But now the question must be asked: What, properly speaking, is this Catholic reality for the sake of which I want to remain a Catholic theologian?

Who Is a Catholic Theologian?

In accordance with the original meaning of the word and with ancient tradition, any theologians can describe themselves as Catholic if they are aware of being obliged in their theology to the "Catholic" — that is, to the *"whole,"* the "universal, comprehensive, total" — Church. This catholicity has two dimensions: temporal and spatial.

First, *catholicity in time:* Theologians are Catholic if they are aware of being united with the whole Church — that is, with the Church of all times. They will therefore not describe from the outset certain centuries as "un-Christian" or "unevangelical." They are sure that in every century there was a community of believers who listened to the gospel of Jesus Christ and tried in one way or other, so far as it is possible for human beings in their frailty and fallibility, to live according to his example.

Protestant radicalism on the other hand (not to be confused with evangelical radicality) is always in danger of wanting unhistorically to begin at zero and so to pass from Jesus to Paul, from Paul to Augustine, and then in a great leap to pass over the Middle Ages to Luther and Calvin, and from that point to leap across one's own "orthodox" tradition to the more recent church fathers or, better, heads of schools.

Catholic theologians, by contrast, will always start out from the fact that there was never a time when the gospel was left without witness and they will try to learn from the Church of the past. While insisting on the necessity of critical scrutiny, they will never overlook the boundary posts and danger signals which the Church in former times, in its concern and struggle for the one true faith, often at times of great distress and danger, set up in the form of creeds and definitions to distinguish between good and bad interpretations of the message. They will never

16

neglect the positive and negative experiences of their family in theology, those teachers who are their older and more experienced fellow students in the school of sacred Scripture. It is precisely in this critical scrutiny that Catholic theologians are interested in the *continuity* which is preserved through all disruptions.

Second, *catholicity in space:* Theologians are Catholic if they are aware of being united with the Church of all nations and continents. They must therefore not orient themselves only to the church of this country or to a national church and will not isolate themselves from the Church as a whole. They are sure that in all nations and on all continents there is a community of believers who in the last resort want nothing other than their own church, a community which is driven no less than the local church by the gospel and which itself has something to say for this local church and its theology.

Protestant particularism on the other hand (not to be confused with evangelical congregational attachment) will always be inclined to orient itself to the locally restricted church, its faith, and its life, and to be content with a theological (occasionally intellectual, highly cultivated) provincialism.

Catholic theologians will always start out from the fact that the gospel has not left itself without witness to any nation, any class or race, and they will try to learn from other churches. However deeply rooted they may be in a particular local church, they will not tie their theology to a particular nation, culture, race, class, form of society, ideology, or school. Precisely in their specific loyalty, Catholic theologians are interested in the *universality* of the Christian faith embracing all groups.

It is in this twofold sense then that I want to be and remain a Catholic theologian and to defend the truth of the Catholic faith in Catholic depth and breadth. And there is no doubt that a number of those who describe themselves as Protestant or evangelical can be and are in fact catholic in this sense, particularly in Tübingen. There ought to be joy at this, even on the part of the institutional Church.

The Criterion of What Is Catholic

Does this affirmation of what is Catholic in time and space, depth and breadth, mean that you have to accept more or less *everything* that has been officially taught, ordered, and observed in the course of twenty centuries? Is it such a total identification that is meant by the Vatican Congregation for the Doctrine of the Faith and the German Bishops Conference when they speak of the "complete," "full," "uncurtailed" truth of the Catholic faith?

Surely what is meant cannot be such a totalitarian conception of truth. For, even on the part of the institutional Church, it is now scarcely disputed that momentous and even theologically "justified" errors have occurred in the history of Catholic teaching and practice and have been corrected (most tacitly) up to a point even by the popes. The list is immense and includes the excommunication of the Ecumenical Patriarch of Constantinople and of the Greek Church, prohibition of vernacular liturgy, condemnation of Galileo and the modern scientific worldview, condemnation of Chinese and Indian forms of divine worship and names of God, the maintenance of the medieval secular power of the pope up to the First Vatican Council with the aid of all the secular and spiritual means of excommunication, condemnation of human rights and particularly freedom of conscience and religion, and discrimination against the Jewish people; finally, in the present century, the numerous condemnations of modern historical-critical exegesis (with reference to the authenticity of the books of the Bible, source criticism, historicity, and literary genres) and condemnations in the dogmatic field, especially in connection with "modernism" (the theory of evolution, understanding of development of dogma); and, in very present times, Pius XII's cleaning-up measures (likewise dogmatically justified) leading to the dismissal of the most outstanding theologians of the preconciliar period such as M. D. Chenu, Yves Congar, Henri de Lubac, Pierre Teilhard de Chardin, who almost all became conciliar theologians under John XXIII.

Is it not obvious that a distinction must be made, precisely for the sake of what is truly Catholic? Not everything that has been officially taught and practiced in the Catholic Church is Catholic. Is it not true that catholicity would harden into "Catholicism" if that which has "become the Catholic reality" (the words are those of Joseph Cardinal Ratzinger of Munich) is simply accepted instead of being submitted to a criterion? And for the Catholic Christian too this criterion can be nothing but the Christian message, the *gospel* in its ultimate concrete form, *Jesus Christ himself*, who for the Church and — despite all assertions to the contrary — also for me is the Son and Word of God. He is and remains the norm in the light of which every ecclesiastical authority — and this is not disputed — must be judged: the norm by which theologians must be tested and in the light of which they must continually justify themselves in the spirit of self-criticism and true humility.

All this means that to be "Catholic" does not imply — for the sake of a supposed "fullness," "integrity," "completeness," "uncurtailedness" — a false humility obediently accepting *everything*, putting up with *everything*. That would be a fatal pooling of contradictions, a confusion of true and false.

Certainly Protestantism has often been reproached for accepting too

18

little, for making a one-sided selection from the whole. But on the other hand, it is often impossible to avoid reproaching Catholicism for accepting too much: a syncretistic accumulation of heterogeneous, distorted, and occasionally un-Christian, pagan elements. Which is worse: a sin by defect or a sin by excess?

In any case then Catholicity must be critically understood — critically, according to the gospel. Together with the Catholic "and" there must be considered the repeatedly necessary protest of the "alone," without which the "and" can never be meaningful. Reforms — in practice and teaching — must remain possible. For the theologian, this means nothing other than the fact that the Catholic theologian in a genuine sense must be evangelically oriented and conversely that the evangelical theologian in a genuine sense must be oriented in a Catholic way. Admittedly, this makes the theological demarcations objectively and conceptually more complicated than they might seem to be in the light of official doctrinal documents which are often terribly simple and display little catholic depth and breadth. Why then do I remain a Catholic? Precisely because as such I can assert an "evangelical catholicity" concentrated and organized in the light of the gospel, which is nothing but genuine ecumenicity. Being Catholic, then, means ecumenical in the fullest sense.

But what of the Roman factor?

"Roman Catholic" is a late and misleading neologism. Once again, I have nothing against Rome. I mean that precisely because I wanted to be a Catholic theologian, I could not tie my Catholic faith and Catholic theology simply to the ingrown Roman absolutist claims from the Middle Ages and later times. Certainly, there must be development in doctrine and practice, but only an *evolutio secundum evangelium*, or "a development in accordance with the gospel." An *evolutio praeter evangelium*, or "a development apart from the gospel," may be tolerated. But an *evolutio contra evangelium*, "a development contrary to the gospel," must be resisted. Applied to the papacy, this means that I have always acknowledged and defended the pastoral primacy of the bishops of Rome linked to Peter and the great Roman tradition as an element in Catholic tradition that is supported by the gospel. But Roman legalism, centralism, and triumphalism in teaching, morality, and church discipline, dominant especially from the eleventh century onward, but prepared long before then, are supported neither by the ancient Catholic tradition nor — still less — by the gospel itself; they were also disavowed by the Second Vatican Council. On the contrary, these things were mainly responsible for the schism with the East and with the Reformation churches. They represent the "Catholicism" about which the present controversy is being carried on in the name of the catholicity of the Catholic Church.

Are there some of our cardinals and bishops who do not want to see that in individual points in theory and practice their thinking is more Roman than Catholic? Perhaps my Protestant colleague, Walther von Löwenich, an authority on both Luther and modern Catholicism, has rightly seen this in the infallibility debate when he writes: "The essential question in the Küng case is not appropriately stated as 'Is Küng still a Catholic?' It should be, 'Will Catholicism struggle out of its dogmatic constriction into genuine catholicity?'"

Catholicity then is gift and task, indicative and imperative, origin and future. It is within this tension that I want to continue the pursuit of theology and as decisively as hitherto to make the message of Jesus Christ intelligible to people of the present time, while being ready to learn and to be corrected whenever it is a question of discussion between equal partners in a fraternal spirit. I must insist, against all the repeated assertions to the contrary by the German bishops, that I have never refused such a discussion even in regard to the Roman authorities, and that I have frequently had this kind of discussion both with representatives of the German Bishops Conference and with the local bishop. But, for the sake of protecting human and Christian rights and for the sake of the freedom of theological science, I have had to resist throughout all the years an interrogation of an Inquisition according all rights to itself and practically none to the accused person. That much I owe to those also who have suffered — and, as it seems, will suffer in the future — under these inhumane and un-Christian measures.

Catholic Church yes! Roman Inquisition, no!

I know that I am not alone in this controversy about true catholicity. I shall fight against any acquiescence together with the many people who have hitherto supported me. We must continue to work together for a truly Catholic Church that is bound by the gospel. For this, it is worthwhile to remain a Catholic.

3

Catholics and Protestants:
An Ecumenical Inventory

We hear complaints in the churches today that an increasing number of Christians are not at ease in any of the Christian churches and tend to form a kind of "third denomination," without attachment to a church. But how are we to cope with this ecclesial "homelessness" if the churches themselves are not becoming more impartial, more flexible, more hospitable also toward each other? For most people today the denominational differences arising from the Reformation have become completely irrelevant. Formerly Catholics knew Protestants only from hearsay and vice versa, while now the members of different denominations are in more or less close contact with one another. Under these circumstances many Christians ascribe the maintenance of the schism to unenlightened, inflexible ecclesiastics and their theologians intent on retaining power. Are they completely wrong in this opinion?

Certainly we cannot ignore *what has hitherto been achieved*. A survey of the ecumenical movement provides scarcely a hint of the labor, tenacity, hope against hope, which were necessary for decades in order merely to get the World Council of Churches established (1948). From a survey of Catholic ecumenism also we can only surmise what efforts and personal sacrifice it cost a few Catholic laypeople and theologians, undaunted by the antiecumenical attitude of the popes up to Pius XII, to prepare for the breakthrough of the Catholic Church to ecumenicity under John XXIII and the Second Vatican Council (1962–65).

It is due to all these untiring efforts — against the background of cruel nationalistic experiences of "Christian" peoples in two world wars — that relations between the churches claiming to follow Jesus Christ have been turned into something positive. And if we look even further back, to the Reformation period, we can see how much the Catholic view of Martin Luther's personality has changed: We can also note the change of temper in Catholic and Protestant "controversial theology": the early polemic gave way to attempts to bring out the differences in the official teaching of the denominations, with the result that subjective polemics were overcome and an "ecumenical" theology emerged. Which means that the churches and their theologies have traveled a long way from denunciation and inquisition to communication and discussion, from denominational coexistence to ecumenical cooperation.

It is true that the Catholic Church in particular has not yet joined the World Council of Churches and presents special difficulties for an ecumenical agreement because of its tradition, teaching, and organization (and especially the primacy and infallibility of the pope). But the fact cannot be overlooked that, in comparison with the post-Tridentine, Counter-Reformation Church — despite all compromises — the basic trend of the Second Vatican Council amounted to a turn of 180 degrees in the direction of ecumenicity. Despite all the remaining unresolved problems (birth control, divorce, ministry, mixed marriages, celibacy, primacy, and infallibility), the concrete *positive results* must not be underestimated. They also provoke *further questions* — to be at least briefly indicated here — to the other churches.

1. Since the Second Vatican Council, what has changed *for Christendom as a whole?*

a. The Catholic *share of guilt* for the schism is now recognized. At the same time the necessity of continual *reform* is accepted: *Ecclesia semper reformanda* — continual renewal of our own Church in life and teaching according to the gospel. But the further question arises: May the other churches then regard themselves as in no need of reform (Orthodox Church) or even as already reformed (Lutheran and Calvinist churches), or are they also still to be reformed?

b. The other Christian communities are *recognized as churches*. In all churches there is a common Christian basis which is perhaps more important than everything that divides them. But again the question arises: Ought there not to be a more intense effort to find the common Christian basis and "substance" also in the other churches?

c. An *ecumenical attitude* is required from the whole Church. There must be an inward conversion of Catholics themselves, a growth of mutual understanding between the churches and a readiness to learn by dialogue, a recognition of the faith, the baptism, the values of other Christians, finally a theology and church history worked out in an ecumenical spirit. But there is a further question: Will the other churches then, for their part, also recognize and realize the numerous Catholic concerns in theology, liturgy, and church structures?

d. *Cooperation* with other Christians is to be promoted in every way. There must be practical collaboration in the whole social field, but also prayer together and increasingly a united worshiping community — especially in the liturgy of the Word — and finally discussion between theologians of equal standing. Here, too, a further question must be faced: Ought not the other churches also develop more strongly a readiness to co-operate?

2. What has changed in regard to the *churches of the Reformation* since the Second Vatican Council? A whole series of concerns which were central to the Reformers have been accepted at least in principle by the Catholic Church.

a. *A new appreciation of the Bible:* (i) In worship: Preaching, prayer, and hymns should all bear the imprint of a biblical spirit; a new and more varied cycle of Scripture readings covering a number of years has been produced. (ii) In the life of the Church as a whole: Instead of insistence on the Latin Vulgate translation there is now a demand for modern translations of the Bible from the original text; instead of the former prohibition of Bible reading by the laity there are now repeated invitations to read the Bible frequently. (iii) In theology: The Church's magisterium is not above God's Word but exists to serve the latter; it is no longer the universal teaching of the Church that revealed truth is contained "partly" in Scripture and "partly" in tradition; the study of Scripture must be the "soul" of theology (and of catechetics), the justification of the historical-critical interpretation of Scripture is recognized, the inerrancy of Scripture is claimed not for statements on natural science but only for truths of salvation.

b. *Genuine people's worship:* the realization of the concerns of the Reformers can be seen in a number of examples: (i) As against the former clerical liturgy, there is a service involving the whole priestly people through an intelligible structure and active participation of the whole congregation in common prayer, singing, and meal. (ii) As against the former proclamation in the alien Latin language, there is a new attention to the Word of God proclaimed in the vernacular. (iii) As against the standardized, uniform Roman liturgy, there is adaptation to the different nations; national episcopates with shared competence instead of the formerly exclusive papal competence. (iv) As against the former proliferation and concealment, there is now simplification and concentration on essentials: revision of all rites and thus a greater similarity between the Mass and the last supper of Jesus. (v) There is reform also of the liturgy

23

of the sacraments, of the church year, of the breviary. (vi) Included in all this is a positive settlement of classical points of controversy (vernacular and the chalice for the laity are likewise permitted in principle).

c. *Revaluation of the laity:* Direct access of the laity to the Scriptures and the realization of popular worship are themselves an important fulfillment of this third concern of the Reformers. In addition, there are numerous theological publications on the importance of the laity in the Church, with an implicit criticism of clericalism; every bishop is expected to set up a pastoral council consisting of priests and laypeople.

d. *Adaptation of the Church to the nations:* As against a centralized system, the importance of the local churches and the particular churches (dioceses, nations) is stressed; national and continental conferences of bishops are to promote practical decentralization; the Roman curia itself is to be internationalized.

e. *Reform of popular piety:* There has been a reform of fasting regulations, of indulgences and devotional practices. Restrictions have been imposed on the excesses of Marian devotion (the Second Vatican Council set up clear limits in this respect by rejecting a separate document on Mary); nor was any additional Marian dogma promulgated.

This largely completed realization of the concerns of the Reformers again raises further questions: Should not the Protestant churches now make it their business to approach Catholics effectively with more self-critical understanding? To put it quite concretely:

- appreciation of the Bible, certainly: but where does Protestantism stand in regard to its neglect of the common tradition of the early Church and of the Middle Ages?

- genuine liturgy of the Word and people's worship, certainly: but what of the celebration of the Eucharist, thrust into the background or even practically excluded in Protestant churches?

- revaluation of the laity, certainly: but what of the importance of ordination and the Church's ministry (also beyond the limits of a particular region)?

- adaptation to the nations, certainly: but what of the international and universal character of the Church, so often put in question by Protestant provincialism?

- reform of popular piety, certainly: but what of the closeness of the Church and its worship to the people, often imperiled by Protestant intellectualism?

3. What has changed in regard to the *Eastern churches*, which have often been regarded as merely an appendage of the Latin Church?

Since Vatican II the churches of the East have been expressly recognized as enjoying equal rights with those of the West. Rebaptism is not required of Orthodox Christians who become Catholics, nor are Orthodox priests expected to be reordained, and celibacy is not imposed on them. If they want to do so, Orthodox Christians may receive the sacraments in Catholic churches; on the other hand, if no Catholic priest is available, Catholics may receive the sacraments in Orthodox churches. Mixed marriages between Catholics and Orthodox are valid, even if they are not contracted in Catholic churches. Ought not all these things to hold also with reference to the Protestant churches? Immediately before the close of the Council there took place simultaneously in Rome and Constantinople the solemn revocation of the mutual excommunication of 1054, which had inaugurated the schism between East and West, lasting almost a thousand years. But does not this very act require both sides to face its consequences, particularly in regard to the eucharistic community? The Orthodox churches remained far too static, rigidly holding to the position not of the primitive Church but of the Byzantine centuries. Ought not they also to have roused themselves to a serious reform of their liturgy, theology, and church structures? But on the other hand the Catholic Church rigidly upheld the primacy of jurisdiction and papal infallibility in its relations with the Orthodox churches. Shouldn't we honestly re-examine both questions in the light of the New Testament and the common early church tradition, instead of refusing to discuss these points of doctrine?

In fact, as even Pope Paul VI has admitted, the *papacy* with its absolute claim is the main difficulty in the way of ecumenical agreement. But is an agreement on this subject at all possible? Yes, if (a) papal *primacy* is understood less as a primacy of honor or jurisdiction and more as a pastoral primacy in the service of the unity of the Church as a whole; (b) papal infallibility is understood as the function of witnessing and proclaiming in the service of the "infallibility" or, better, "indefectibility" — that is, of the indestructibility — of the Church in truth, despite all errors in detail.

The rest of the doctrinal differences with reference to Scripture and tradition, grace and justification, Church and sacraments may be regarded as largely settled in theological terms. The situation can be summed up briefly and systematically. Today the primacy of *Scripture* as the original Christian testimony (normative norm) prior to all later *tradition* is acknowledged also by Catholic theology and, on the other hand, the importance of postbiblical tradition (regulated norm) is admitted at least in principle by Protestant theology. Justification by faith alone is affirmed by Catholic theologians, just as the necessity of works or deeds of love is affirmed by Protestant theologians.

Fortunately, much more has happened among the ordinary people in the churches. Mutual understanding today in a large number of Catholic, Protestant, and Orthodox congregations has increased to an extent formerly inconceivable. There is intercommunion already among many groups. This actually living ecumenicity at the base is more important for the future than all theological controversies and all finely spun ecclesiastical diplomacy. Nevertheless, more intensive support for ecumenical efforts must be expected from the leadership of the churches, particularly in regard to urgent *ecumenical imperatives* such as (a) reform and mutual recognition of church ministries, (b) common liturgy of the Word and open communion, (c) common building and common use of churches and other structures, (d) common fulfillment of service to society, (e) increasing integration of theological faculties and religious instruction, (f) drawing up of concrete plans for union on the part of church leaders at national and universal levels.

Ecumenicity is more than mere activism in reform. It can be found and realized only if all the churches concentrate afresh on the one Christian tradition, on the gospel of Jesus Christ himself. Only in that light can denominational fears and uncertainties be reduced, ideological fanaticism and bitter prejudice be overcome, the economic, political, cultural entanglements with a particular society, social stratum, class, race, or state concealed behind theological differences be discerned, and an advance be made toward a new freedom. This of course means that there can be no ecumenical agreement without renewal in the Church, but also no renewal in the Church without ecumenical agreement.

But what then is "Catholic" and what is "Protestant"? In the future the differences will continue to find expression only in diverse traditional *basic attitudes* which have developed from the time of the Reformation but can be integrated today into a true ecumenicity.

a. What is *Catholic?* Someone who attaches special importance to the Catholic — that is, *entire*, universal, all-encompassing, total — Church. Concretely, to the *continuity* of faith in time and the community of faith in space, maintained in all disruptions.

b. Who is *Protestant?* Someone who attaches special importance in all tradition, doctrines, and practices of the Church to constant, critical recourse to the gospel (Scripture) and to constant, practical *reform* according to the norm of the gospel.

c. But from all this it is clear that "Catholic" and Protestant" basic attitudes, correctly understood, are by no means mutually exclusive. Today even the "born" Catholic can be truly Protestant and the "born"

26

Protestant truly Catholic in their mentality, so that even now in the whole world there are innumerable Christians who — despite the obstructions of the churches' machinery — do in fact realize a genuine ecumenicity finding its center in the light of the gospel. Being truly Christian today means being an *ecumenical Christian*.

Such an ecumenical Church of the future certainly must not dissolve into disparate, unorganized groups. But, despite the fact that it must also have an institutional character, it would not be a single-party organization, an absolutist religious Roman Empire. This ecumenical Church of the future would be marked by more truthfulness, freedom, humanity, by more broad-mindedness, tolerance, and magnanimity, more Christian self-confidence, supreme composure, and courage to think and to decide. Such a Church would not always be behind the times but as far as possible ahead of them. It might be the avant-garde of a better humanity.

Part Two —

Overcoming
Polarization

4 —

Parties in the Church?

The question is given different answers for different periods (New Testament, early Church, Middle Ages, Reformation, present) by different academic disciplines (politics and sociology, exegesis and history, systematic and pastoral theology) and by members of different confessions (Orthodox, Lutheran, Reformed, Anglican, Free Church, Catholic). Individual emphases vary widely.

A comprehensive and generally convincing answer seems difficult. On the other hand, the present distress of the churches in general and of the Catholic Church in particular calls for urgent efforts to examine and compare the conclusions of political scientists, exegetes, historians, theologians, and practitioners of every stripe, to see if a consensus already exists or is at least in sight.

Defining the Problem

1. *Parties in the Church are a real problem.*

We fully expected some of the contributors to reject the problem of parties in the Church, either because they thought that it did not exist in some churches now or in the early or medieval Church or because the question was simply unacceptable on theological grounds, parties in the Church being *a priori* a sin against the unity of the Church.

In this article Küng summarizes the discussion of the contributors to *Concilium* vol. 88, *Polarization in the Church*, edited by H. Küng and W. Kasper (New York: Herder and Herder, 1973). The contributors included O. Chadwick, M.-D. Chenu, T. Eschenburg, T. Hesburgh, O. Kéramé, R. Modras, N. Nissiotis, D. O'Hanlon, R. Pesch, P. Potter, K. E. Skydsgaard, L.-J. Suenens, W. Visser't Hooft, and H.-J. Vogt.

In fact, all the contributors, however they see the solution, agree that parties in the Church are a real problem. Indeed, the specialists in this sphere (Suenens, Visser't Hooft, Potter, Hesburgh) point out or take for granted that we are facing new polarizations in the Church. New tensions in the churches have replaced old tensions between the churches. These new tensions are problematical, but they also reveal new possibilities for ecumenism (Visser't Hooft, Skydsgaard, Nissiotis, Potter, O'Hanlon, Modras, referring to sociological research). Even in the Catholic Church which, in the period from the Counter-Reformation to Vatican II, had a monolithic structure, strong polarizations and parties in one form or another are at least possible. The word "party" is used here in the broad sense of "tendency," "movement," "group," or "wing," whereas in the section below "A Systematic Solution Today" it will be used in the narrower sense of "political" party.

2. *The question is sharpened by the convergence of theological and sociological approaches.*

From the point of view of theology, the Church has a special commitment to unity. This is stressed by all the contributors. Because of its basic Christian program, the Christian community cannot accept barriers of class, race, culture, or education, but attempts instead to include tensions and contradictions (Skydsgaard) that are socio-political ("master-slave"), cultural ("Greek-barbarian"), and sexual ("man-woman"). This all-embracing unity is already basically achieved and manifested in eucharistic communion (Nissiotis). From the point of view of sociology, however, the Church is also a human organization and not exempt from the sociological laws which bind all human organizations (Eschenburg, Chadwick, Nissiotis, Modras, O'Hanlon), and for this reason the possibility of parties in the Church cannot be excluded in advance.

In its sharpest form, the question runs as follows: Can a community whose aim is to embrace and transcend parties in society, including modern political parties, admit parties within itself, ecclesial parties?

3. *Theological, liturgical, and disciplinary pluralism in the Church is legitimate.*

There is also false unity (Skydsgaard). Pluralism can be a source of freedom and creativity in the Church. The diamond of Christian truth has many facets; difference is not bad, only difference hardened into exclusiveness (Suenens). Since the Second Vatican Council, the need and value of a complex pluralism is no longer disputed even within the Catholic Church, but vigorously affirmed: diversity in teaching, liturgy, and organization, arising out of diversity in language, culture, and ways of thought, philosophical and cultural categories, different religious experiences, and different selections from the New Testament (Modras,

Hesburgh, Potter). On all sides, and most strongly from the Eastern (Nissiotis, Kéramé) and Anglican churches (Chadwick), there is a desire, not for a uniform, but for a pluriform Church.

In this quarter, then, there are no obstacles to allowing the application to the Church of terms such as "movement," "group," "tendency," and "wing." Parties (in the broad sense) in the Church·are acceptable without qualification (and even to some extent desirable) when this term covers groups which differ from each other and are not in conflict, but in communion with each other. These movements may be missionary, biblical, liturgical, or catechetical. They may be movements for peace and justice, national, ethnic, racial, and social groupings, different religious orders or communities, associations and organizations of all sorts. There will be room in the Church of the future for "parties" which bring a variety of groups into fruitful interaction and yet maintain community among them (O'Hanlon, Nissiotis, Chadwick).

4. *Pluralism in the Church has limits.*

Pluralism can be a danger to the unity and continued existence of the Church. Today Protestants too stress more than they did in the past the need for the unity of the Church in the face of so many attempts to further particular interests in the Church (Skydsgaard, Visser't Hooft). Eastern Christians encourage the formation of groupings in the Church, provided that they do not separate from the mother-church and set themselves up as churches (Nissiotis). Even the Anglican Church, which openly accepts parties, has some limits — a church in which all possible views could be taught would not be the Church of Christ (Chadwick). Indifferent pluralism would destroy the character of the Church as the community of believers. Pluralism may be accepted, but promiscuity is rejected. A community that wants to survive needs at least a minimum consensus (Modras, Suenens). Just as democracy cannot be abolished in the name of democracy, neither can the plural Church in the name of ecclesial pluralism.

However much the Church may tolerate various movements, groups, tendencies, and wings, there is general agreement that it cannot tolerate sects which cut themselves off from it. Definitely unacceptable (and indeed harmful, even if not always easy to eliminate) are parties in the Church which seal themselves off and separate themselves from the community and its faith and life. These parties include all sects, in other words, whether they are based on theology, race, or culture. In the Church of the future there can therefore be no parties which bring alienation and dissension into the church community (O'Hanlon).

5. *The final criterion of unity and plurality in the Church is Jesus Christ himself.*

Because of this ambiguity, because many parties are neither definitely acceptable nor definitely unacceptable, but a question, because parties can exist in the Church which remain in community with each other but are also in conflict, further clarification is necessary (O'Hanlon). Notwithstanding any political commitment on the part of the Church or its members, a political ideology, whether Marxist or capitalist, Communist or Fascist, can never be the decisive criterion for the church community (Nissiotis). The decisive criterion for the church community, for the necessary unity and possible plurality, can for the Church of Jesus Christ be only Jesus Christ himself, as the New Testament testifies. Today this point is stressed equally by Catholics (Suenens, Modras, O'Hanlon), Orthodox (Nissiotis), and Protestants (Visser't Hooft, Skydsgaard, Potter), even if it is expressed in different words. Examples of this are "the person and mission of Jesus," "the gospel of Jesus Christ," "the Lord of the Church," which is the "Body of Christ." If, then, the norm for the Church as the community of those who believe in Christ is Christ himself, clearly all dogmas, rites, and organizational forms, and all theologies and structures, must be open to reform and correction. *Ecclesia semper reformanda* of course presupposes *Ecclesia semper eadem* (Modras, Chadwick), reform without a change of identity.

Principles of a Solution

1. *There are groups in the New Testament which can be called parties.*

The Judaism of Jesus' time was already familiar with religious parties. Best known are the *haireseis* or "parties" of the Sadducees, Pharisees, and Nazarites, groups which took an individual position on certain important religious questions, without renouncing their allegiance to Judaism like the heretical (in the negative sense) "sect" of the Samaritans (Pesch).

Therefore the Church, too, which is based on Jesus Christ, has from the beginning existed in various groups, which in contemporary terminology may certainly be called "parties" (*haireseis*) because they were based on different "teachings." The primitive Jerusalem community had "Hebrews" and "Hellenists," and later the exclusively Jewish Christian group in Jerusalem took a harder line and insisted on observance of the Jewish law by all. The Antioch group regarded the Jewish law as abolished in Christ and practiced a mission to the Gentiles which ignored the law. There were also further distinctions between the stricter (James) and more liberal (Peter) Jewish Christians, between communities willing to compromise (James's Antioch formula) and the uncompromising apostle Paul, in whose communities old and perhaps also new parties emerged (though in Corinth they may have been not so much theological parties as factions which grew up around particular individuals on personal grounds).

2. *These parties are not so much the result of human sin as of the preaching of the gospel in a diverse socio-cultural context.*

It was inevitable that the preaching of the gospel to all nations and all people should have different results — particularly as regards the form of the preaching and observance of the Jewish law — in areas of traditional Jewish thought and in the wide area of Hellenistic Judaism in the diaspora. These groupings led to party spirit, opposition and tension in theory and practice which was probably just as strong as what we know today (Pesch, Modras, Visser't Hooft, Potter).

3. *Nevertheless the individual communities remained linked in a unity which did not allow a division in the Church.*

The foundation of this unity was confession of one God and one Lord, Jesus Christ, and thus one faith, one baptism, and one Lord's Supper. Even the uncompromising Paul warned against divisions (*schismata*), appealed for a common mind, and was in word and deed in the forefront of the fight for the unity of his communities among themselves and with Jerusalem. "Is Christ divided?" was his battle-cry. Nevertheless, right from the beginning this unity was not a matter of uniformity, but consisted in communication between Christian groups, the transmission of different theological traditions, the adaptation of attitudes and argument about Jesus Christ, the standard of faith, who was not the permanent possession of any one group but was constantly having to be rediscovered in new situations (Pesch, Modras, Potter).

4. *As well as the different parties within the church community, there were groups which not only interpreted the gospel differently but preached a different gospel.*

To be distinguished from the parties within the Church are the true sects, *haireseis* in the firmly negative sense, which shut themselves up in their own tradition and language and do not communicate with the church community. Not only Paul, but other writers of the New Testament and several Apostolic Fathers, attack such separatist groups (Pesch).

5. *According to the New Testament, the existence of parties in the Church is permitted, not for the sake of divisions, but for the increase of commitment to the Lord and his Church.*

The formation of groups is permitted and desired as an aid to unity and communication, for the building up of the community and for mission, and especially for the service of people. The existence of parties of

35

this type with a special commitment gives groups a more definite character but does not destroy unity. It promotes toleration within the Church but does not make it more difficult to excommunicate those who reject communication in the Church (Pesch).

The Lesson of History

1. *Throughout the whole history of the Church there have been tendencies, movements, groups, and wings.*

These groups have tended toward theology or social affairs, church politics or spirituality. There have also been, from the beginning, groups which, because they have emphasized a particular interest, have separated themselves from or have been forced out of the Church (Vogt).

2. *From the fourth century in particular there were in the early medieval Church true parties with a theological basis.*

These were not, as in the past, groups with a particular theology sharply distinguished from the Church as a whole. Now the whole episcopate was divided into changing groups which defended their positions with propaganda literature, by furthering special interests, or by mutual accusation and changing coalitions. The struggle centered on the filling of episcopal appointments. Nevertheless a permanent secession by large groups was avoided in the fourth century (Vogt).

3. *A common concern can be seen behind the various contradictory theological formulations.*

Of great importance for the preservation of church unity amid all the party struggles was the conciliatory policy of various bishops, and especially Athanasius, who avoided blind partiality and never lost sight of the issue which lay behind and beyond disputed formulas. In this way the various parties were able to recognize the different terminology of other parties as possible and legitimate, and no more was asked than acceptance of the Nicene Creed and condemnation of the old heresies. And these parties had positive as well as negative results — they contributed to a more comprehensive understanding of the truth. Not only heretical isolationism, but also ultra-orthodox zeal, has often held up the discovery of truth and inflicted fruitless party battles on the Church (Vogt, Modras).

4. *In the complexity of the historical situation, it is difficult to discern the boundary between the true faith and heresy, between a party within the Church and a sect.*

Both in the teaching and practice of the Church actual historical situations include an infinity of tendencies and divergences, affinities and tensions, connections and distinctions. Concealed rigorism and reconciled heresy, influence, aggression, and delicate balancing factors make a judgment difficult. The ambiguity of the word *hairesis* reflects the ambiguity of situations (Chenu).

5. *Especially since the High Middle Ages, it has been impossible to ignore the socio-economic influences on many movements, parties, and even divisions in the Church.*

There can be no neat separation between Church and society, theology and politics. Neither churches nor sects, faith or heresy, can be analyzed without taking into account their social roots. There is what might be called a sociological justification for heresy. Economic prosperity, the development of free towns and independent universities, the new ideas of class and increased mobility have influenced ecclesiastical and theological parties just as, conversely, the religious appeal to the people, the gospel for the poor, the idea of brotherhood, the new ethos of work and apocalyptic expectations have influenced social developments and divisions. Evangelical and political movements have often run side by side and they have always depended and reacted on each other, often with mutual confusion (Chenu).

6. *An authoritarian Church provokes opposition from within.*

From the High Middle Ages onward, a very diverse opposition grew up on the part of individuals and groups. It had a socio-economic as well as a spiritual and theological character, and directed itself against a hierarchy which had identified itself with the feudal system and had thereby become rich and authoritarian (Chenu). How dangerous this often ambivalent appeal to the gospel and new social factors was to become did not become clear until the Late Middle Ages and the Reformation.

7. *The split between East and West was essentially the result of a rejection of the pluralism traditionally practiced in the united Church.*

Unity in the Western Church came increasingly to be understood as uniformity. This led not only to an internal hardening but also external isolationism, in the form of a slow drift away from the Eastern churches, which finally became a breach which has still not been mended. The existence of Eastern churches which differ in form among themselves and have an equal claim with Rome to direct apostolic origin is a challenge to the Western Church, and in particular to the papacy, to rethink plurality in the teaching, liturgy, and constitution of the Church and to make room for it in genuinely collegial structures (Kéramé).

8. *Luther saw himself as a reformer within the Church, but was forced to accept a division in the Church for the sake of the gospel.*

There can be historical moments in which criticism must be expressed and protest registered in the sharpest possible way. Luther did not want a breach in the community of the Church, but he did want obedience to the gospel. Since this controversy was clearly about essential elements of the

Christian message, the result was not the secession of a fringe group but a split, this time down the middle of the Western Church. Parties within the Church became two different expressions of the Christian Church. To this extent we can talk of a "hierarchy of parties," parties based on superficial matters and those based on essentials (Skydsgaard).

9. *The existence of parties within a single church (as notably in the Anglican) is assessed differently even within this church.*

The Anglican Church gradually came to be divided into three parties, high, low, and broad church. What was still regarded in the seventeenth century as a necessary evil or even sin has since the nineteenth century been regarded as an advantage and an advance, though there have always been protests from Anglo-Catholics. In our own century the Anglican Church has often been put forward as a model of what ecumenical efforts should aim at, as a "bridge church" between different tendencies. However, this argument has not been generally accepted either inside or outside the Anglican Church (Chadwick).

A Systematic Solution Today

1. *Current terminology is dominated by the concept of political party (i.e., "party" in the narrower sense).*

"Party" in the narrower sense does not today mean a separatist sect, but neither does it mean merely a tendency, movement, or group ("party" in the broad sense). A party in the narrower sense has the following characteristics. It seeks to take over and exercise political power, to achieve specific aims in social welfare and prevent others from being achieved. It puts forward programs and candidates for elections and has a permanent organization (Eschenburg).

2. *Whether such parties should be formed in the Church is not a dogmatic, but primarily a political question.*

The history of political parties and their origin is closely connected with the development of the franchise and its extension to broader sections of the population. Where elections are allowed, the formation of parties is a normal development, and they have always been concerned with putting up candidates for parliamentary assemblies and winning elections. As a rule, every parliament has formal groupings (for the orderly conduct of debates and divisions) and parties (at least for electoral purposes). The setting up of collegial or synodal bodies in the Catholic Church in parishes and dioceses, at the national and (on a limited scale) the universal level, with at least some elected members therefore makes it possible to form organized groups within these bodies and parties for elections to them (Eschenburg, O'Hanlon).

Acceptance or rejection of parties in the narrower sense does, of course, have theological implications. On the one hand, for example, it makes the priesthood of all believers a reality and, on the other, it preserves church unity. But the question as to whether these theological goals should be attained by means of ecclesiastical parties or without them is a practical question (O'Hanlon, Eschenburg). In answering it, however, the political implications of such parties must be borne in mind. There is, for example, a need for an efficient party organization and at least a rudimentary bureaucracy and party propaganda. Members have to be recruited and party activities have to be financed. Parties may acquire a momentum of their own and this can be regulated by the parent organization (in this case the Church) only to a limited degree (Eschenburg).

3. *There are arguments for parties in the Church.*

Organized parties in the Church would make it possible: (a) for the laity to share responsibility without the present feeling of impotence and frustration; (b) to settle, in an orderly and public way, the conflicts which cannot be avoided in any healthy society, on the basis of shared convictions and ideals; (c) to educate church members through the information and discussion which goes with the existence of parties. This is of particular importance in a time of rapid social change in the Church and pressure for it to adapt to new situations (O'Hanlon).

4. *There are arguments against parties in the Church.*

Organized parties in the Church would make it possible: (a) for particular religious differences to become institutions, be made absolute, and be perpetuated; (b) for permanent hostility to arise between persons and groups, a weakening, perhaps leading to the collapse of communications between the parties and giving rise to new divisions in the Church; (c) for Church parties to be confused with political parties and systems, which vary so widely in different countries (O'Hanlon).

5. *In particular situations the formation of parties or at least of groups may be unavoidable.*

Since the situations in different countries, with different political systems and levels of development, are extremely varied, it is hardly possible to suggest a general solution (O'Hanlon). In the past, an authoritarian and undemocratic church system has often given rise to a sharp polarization, the formation of parties, and even divisions (Kéramé, Chenu) and this may happen again today. Above all, the connection of ecclesiastical authority with established political power and its refusal to accept political or social commitment may lead to the formation of groups engaged in contestation (Nissiotis). Sometimes, as the result of particular traditions and dispositions of power, a particular group uses spiritual (and also legal and financial) power as a subtle or sometimes even brutal means to maintain a status quo advantageous to itself and to prevent serious reforms in Church and society. This one-party church is not the best advertisement for unity and order in the Church.

In this way the formation of a group, or eventually an organized party, within the Church may be unavoidable. For example, when bishops in a synod form a bloc, a counter-bloc is almost always formed, and this will in time have effects on the situation in the Church outside the synod. When a central Roman administration attempts to restore its feudal and absolutist power over the Church's teaching and practice in a democratic age, sharp polarizations, internal disaffection of large sections of the population from Rome, and open conflicts are to be expected.

6. *If possible, organized groups and parties in the Church should be avoided.*

From a political point of view, it is not certain whether the advantages to the Church and humanity of group and party formation outweigh the disadvantages (O'Hanlon). Certainly the tactics, propaganda, and the campaigning methods used by political parties can hardly be a model for the Church (Eschenburg).

From the theological point of view, it is appropriate that a community whose aim is to embrace and transcend social antagonisms and political parties should not add its own (inter-church or intra-church) antagonisms to those of society. In some circumstances these take the form of hot or cold wars of religion. It is better for a community of faith, love, and prayer to express its spiritual unity as free agreement and mutual openness (Potter).

In view of the well-known inadequacies of the political party system, it may be possible to find other, no less effective, models of decision-making for the Church which are more appropriate to it (O'Hanlon). Questions of faith can hardly be solved by purely majority decisions. In any case decisions in church synods have usually been sought through consensus — not a mathematical but moral unanimity — which means leaving disputed questions open. Even during Vatican II, though votes were necessary, efforts were made to reach this sort of unanimity and in spite of the variety of tendencies no parties or fixed groups in the end emerged. As a means of avoiding the undesirable developments of the party system, there might be practical and legal advantages in having direct voting for specific candidates instead of a proportional system with party lists. In this system the fundamental choice could be limited to the local community or small region, and representatives to the synods chosen from the local and regional assemblies.

7. Pluralism between churches could become pluralism within the Church.

Even if the formation of groups and parties in the churches is often unavoidable in practice, the terrible experiences of the past make it vital to avoid fundamental divisions in the Church — even for the sake of the gospel. The unfortunate handling by both sides of the Reformation should not be taken by either side as a model for future cases.

The old days must not return. Today all the various churches seek together and concentrate on the essence of the gospel as a means to give scope to the diversity of understanding of the one gospel (Skydsgaard, Potter). Ecumenism is indivisible. It applies *ad intra* and *ad extra*, and must start in its own church if it wants to enlighten the *oikoumenē* (Visser't Hooft). We should work toward a situation in which distinctions between Catholics, Orthodox, Anglicans, and Protestants of various tendencies become parties or tendencies within the Church, groups which are different, but no longer far apart, but rather in full community with each other (Modras, O'Hanlon). At this stage a common celebration of the Lord's Supper by the different churches should be considered (Skydsgaard). At the same time, and with an eye to the more distant future and the other great world religions, the possibility should also be considered of recognizing Hindu Christians and Buddhist Christians with their rich traditions (critically examined) within one Christian Church (O'Hanlon).

What has to be done to overcome polarizations in the churches and between the churches? We must expose ourselves fully to Christ and his gospel and together look at God and our fellow human beings and accept all the consequences of this attitude. We must be open to the Spirit and in sympathy with each other whenever we differ (Hesburgh). We must learn to speak more freely to each other and to listen to each other in vital questions of faith (Potter). We must keep a sense of proportion, which was so characteristic of the first Christian witnesses, have a deeper understanding of the different spiritual gifts with their importance for the life of the Church as against one-sided and exclusive theologies, and take seriously the plurality of cultures and the resulting pluriformity in the expression of the Christian faith (Visser't Hooft). We must try to understand more deeply the conciliar process through which the Church lived in the past and in which it will find new life (Potter). We must practice, together with the priestly ministry of liberating reconciliation, the prophetic ministry of liberating conflict and learn to conquer all conflicts which divide the Church and the nations in the last resort through the Cross of Christ (Potter).

5

For a Church of Renovation
and Innovation

I have been asked to make a brief statement on the situation of the Catholic Church in West Germany. This is not easy, especially when one has been, like me, immediately affected by this situation, and so can scarcely be viewed as a neutral observer. Precisely for that reason I cannot simply present my altogether personal estimate of the situation here. Rather I would like, in an act of gratitude, to make myself a spokesman for the many people who helped me to survive intellectually in this Church at the hardest time. These are the people who spoke out in public for me and who get passed over in silence in the proclamations and documentation issued by the German Bishops Conference, published by Norbert Greinacher and Herbert Haag (*Der Fall Küng: Eine Documentation*, Munich, 1980 [The Küng Case: Documentation]). As opposed to the "Church from above," the official Church, the hierarchy, they represent the contrasting voices of the "Church from below," the community of the Church, the people of God itself.

Three basic insights concerning the future of the Church in West Germany suggest themselves to me from the many testimonies published by Greinacher and Haag, three theses that I now offer for discussion.

A Church of Repression Threatens from Above

By "repression" I understand the crushing of people by people through a specific system and its representatives.

More precisely for the *Church*, there is a threat of limiting and hindering the free development of individual Christians and entire groups through different spiritual (and often political, legal, and financial) instruments of power and manipulating of consciousness. Thus there is a threat from a system that turns free Christian men and women into conformist followers, and in many ways no longer lets the "spiritual" repression even be felt as such.

The *official Roman Catholic Church* naturally tries to create the impression that there is no threat of repression in the Catholic community:

- as if on the pastoral scene a climate of brotherhood and love prevailed;
- as if full freedom of theological research and teaching existed;
- as if ecumenical activity had not come to a standstill, as if there were no alliance between a conservative curia and conservative bishops on the one hand and reactionary political trends on the other.

Still, from the *Catholic Church community* we increasingly hear highly representative voices that attest to the opposite: On all sides — despite all the denials by Rome and the bishops — there is talk about the freeze-up of the Council, about the lack of success of the German synods, about the taking back of newly discovered dimensions of church life, the stagnation of ecumenical understanding, the repression of the new creative freedom and joy in the Catholic Church.

In fact, various events and developments in the last few years have led many people in the Church to fear that their concerns are being disappointed, their commitment is going to naught, their hopes are being downtrodden, that good beginnings are repressed and movements halted, and thus the credibility of the Catholic Church has been shaken internally and externally. Even many responsible members in the Church, pastors, chaplains, parish officials, religion teachers, youth leaders, men and women, are increasingly afraid to say out loud what is moving them: "We admit that we are afraid to say out loud what moves us," says for example the national leadership of the Catholic Youth Community (KJG) in an open letter to the KJG parishes. But, they say, keeping quiet to avoid trouble can be justified only so long as this "does not run counter to our goals." And events since December 18, 1979, the date my canonical mission was cancelled, make the leadership point to the following developments, which spread anxiety and silent conformism:

- We are thinking of the rigorous attitude of Pope John Paul II in the area of Catholic sexual morality, which keeps on disappointing the hopes and expectations of many concerned individuals, who are looking for support and direction instead of regimentation.
- We are thinking of other procedures brought by the Congregation for the Doctrine of the Faith against more theologians (known and unknown investigations).

- We are thinking of the experiences that we in the KJG have had to go through with the German Bishops Conference.

- We are thinking of the most recent measures, regulations, and guidelines for the appointment of church aides; of the methods and procedures for scrutiny, in which the person concerned only rarely learns the whole story.

- We are thinking of the firing of aides from church institutions (hospitals, kindergartens, etc.), which may be legally unassailable, but is not supported by the commandment of love.

- We are thinking of the biased investigations of religion teachers in connection with their church authorization to teach, where the issue is not their academic qualifications, but their compliance with the Church's moral laws.

- We are thinking of the demand for the right to veto spiritual guides for youth groups.

- We are thinking of the efforts to promote and strengthen those groups in the Church from which a critical attitude is not to be expected.

- We are thinking of the countless proceedings in which uncomfortable members of the community are marginalized.

No Revolutionary Church Threatens from Below

By "revolution" I mean a violent overthrow. More precisely for the Church I mean a violent overturning of order in the doctrine, morality, discipline, values, and representatives of the Church, an overthrow that amounts to a "different gospel" and a different Church. The *official Roman Catholic Church* and certain court theologians are actually trying to make it seem

- as if in the Catholic Church community something like a Revolution were threatening, as if the various movements for pastoral renewal and base communities were tending toward an overthrow of the existing Church order;

- as if the theologians were dumping the "deposit" of faith, making "simple" people insecure in their belief and deliberately causing polarization and confrontations;

- as if ecumenical understanding were abandoning essential Catholic teaching;

- as if in Latin America liberation theology and pastoral practice were working for violent political upheaval in all states.

44

Yet from the *Catholic Church community* we increasingly hear quite representative voices that attest to the opposite: Everywhere there is resistance

- against the official Church's method of discrimination and defamation of those members of the Church who differ with reactionary cardinals in Rome and Germany on some points of doctrine, morality, discipline, and politics;

- against the defamation of socially committed Christians — bishops, pastors, theologians, or lay people — in Latin America, whom they try to discredit as Marxists and communists;

- against the defamation of women and even nuns, in the United States for example, who take a stand against the discriminatory treatment of women in the Church and against the ban on the ordination of women;

- against the defamation of moral theologians in America and Europe who speak up for the moral autonomy of today's Christians, for a more understandable morality of sex and marriage, etc.

In West Germany too countless pastors and chaplains, religion teachers, journalists, and theologians, responsible individuals in student communities and youth associations have been forced to experience the un-Christian reaction of the official Church to criticism. To quote once again the national leadership of the Catholic Youth Community: "The responsible persons are defamed and guilt is imputed to them alone. They alone have misused trust and for this reason they are not acceptable. This is how disciplinary measures against individual persons are explained and justified to the public. We ourselves are afraid of this mechanism, and it is the main reason why we have hitherto kept silence."

People who speak in this way are no revolutionaries. They *are* loyal Catholics committed to the Church, who like countless others are a Church and *want* to remain a Church, even if they disagree with certain time-bound doctrinaire notions and practices of certain functionaries. For Vatican II defined the Church as a brotherly community and the people of God. "The proceedings of the German Bishops Conference and the Congregation for the Doctrine of the Faith and the image employed in the Church's public life of the Church as a business with business rules and regulations," says the Theological Advisory Board of the diocese of Rottenburg-Stuttgart, "reduce the Church to a caricature of what it actually is supposed to be." "Nevertheless, "observes the working group of Catholic University Students and College Communities, "we will not let ourselves be driven out of the Church — out of the Church that is not (only) the Church of the Roman prelates, but in the first instance the Church of Jesus Christ."

In the name of all the people concerned I protest here against the branding — again become standard procedure — of every loyal opposition in the Church as heretical. But the Church of Jesus Christ is no totalitarian system. Neither is it an army, based on military obedience, nor a business where the boss is always the boss, nor an association that can simply throw any member out after a violation of the by-laws. The Church of Christ is a community of faith made up of fundamentally equally entitled free children of God, free, grown-up sons and daughters of God, who are all brothers and sisters. "Where the Spirit of the Lord is there is liberty" (2 Cor. 3:17). And "Christ set us free to be free men. Stand firm, then, and refuse to be tied to the yoke of slavery again" (Gal. 5:1) cries Paul — and as far as I know they didn't take away his ecclesiastical teaching license because of that.

We can see some of the hopes and expectations aroused by the Catholic Church of the future in the statement appended to the synodal resolution "Services and Offices" by the professional association of the pastoral advisors to the diocese of Rottenburg-Stuttgart:

> We would like to spend still more imagination and energy on making the saving work of Jesus Christ present in concrete human and social situations. For this we look to the bishops for help in opening up new possibilities and giving less support to the existing order of things.
>
> We wish to champion the pluralism that can exist within belief in the one Lord, and in the process to do everything so that different opinions do not lead to polarization and more opposition. Wherever possible, we wish to try to work for the resolution of conflicts not from the top down. Every Christian who wants to share responsibility for the Church must be given a genuine chance to do so because the Spirit gives everyone the gift and vocation for the building up of the Church of Jesus Christ in the world (see the synodal resolution "Services and Offices," 3.1.1).
>
> We would like to be a Church and to work for a Church that is concerned not with itself but with men and women. For this reason we see it as part of the Church's nature as the people of God to be *on the way* with all seeking, questioning, and doubting persons.

From Below and from Above the Gospel Calls
for a Church of Renovation and Innovation

It should be made quite clear here that we do not want to separate out the "Church from above" and the "Church from below" but to bring them together. Of course, this has to be done in such a way that the bishops — to quote Paul again — "do not dictate the terms of your faith; but work with you for your own happiness" (2 Cor. 1:24).

By "renovation" I mean renewal looking backward: toward the original standard. By "innovation" I mean renewal looking forward: toward the demands of a new future.

More precisely, for the Church I mean a planned-controlled *aggiornamento* (John XXIII) of church teaching, morality, and discipline according to the standard of Jesus Christ himself as attested to in the Scripture. At the same time we must observe the "signs of the times" and enter into the new experiences, needs, and hopes of men and women in critical-creative adoption and application of new ideas, models, and methods in the most varied domains, for the realization of previously unexercised possibilities.

It is well known that the *official Roman Catholic Church* likes to call for penance, preferably from others: from the laity, from the "lower" clergy, from political parties, from society, from "the world" in general. And the guilt for all mistakes and abuses is readily sought in, or presumed to lie with, others. In areas where the official Church ought to change itself, of course, it usually shows itself to be astonishingly unrepentant. It reacts irritably and lovelessly, indeed wherever possible with disciplinary-legal measures of compulsion. There is an unwillingness to repent not only on matters where, owing to its extremely conservative notions, it has a large part of the active members of the Church against it, but even where it blatantly has the gospel of Jesus Christ against it.

When I think of the Church of the future I cannot with the best will in the world imagine that the One whom Christianity invokes would, if he returned, take a position on today's controversial questions like that of the Roman, and often the German, church authorities:

- that he who warned the Pharisees about placing intolerable burdens on people's shoulders would today declare all "artificial" contraception a mortal sin;

- that he who was continually accompanied by women (his support system) and every one of whose apostles — with the exception of Paul — was and remained married would in today's situation forbid marriage to ordained men and ordination to all women;

- that he would in this way increasingly rob the communities of their chaplains and pastors and would offer them substitute Eucharists;
- that he who took the adulteress and sinners under his wing would issue such harsh verdicts on delicate questions and issues that have to be judged in a nuanced-critical fashion, such as premarital intercourse, homosexuality, and abortion. . . .

No, I just can't think that if he returned today, he would have agreed

- when in the ecumenical area confessional differences are upheld as an impediment to marriage, indeed have recently been made an impediment to entrance into pastoral service for Catholic lay theologians (as they are for Protestant aspirants to the ministry);
- when the validity of the ordination and eucharistic celebrations of Protestant pastors was contested;
- when open communion and joint eucharistic celebrations, the common building of churches and parish centers, and ecumenical religious instruction were prevented;
- when instead of convincing Catholic theologians, student pastors, chaplains, religion teachers, journalists, association officials, and other responsible persons by giving reasons, Church authorities tried to tame them with decrees, "declarations," and depriving them of their canonical mission. . . .

Should this be the future of the Church? No, if one wishes to be Christian, one cannot demand freedom and human rights for the Church from the outside while refusing to grant them within. Urgent church reforms in Germany cannot be replaced by grand words about Europe, the Third World, and the North-South conflict at synods, church congresses, and papal rallies. You can't preach justice, peace, and human dignity only in places where it costs the Church and its leadership nothing.

And from the *Catholic Church community* we increasingly hear quite representative voices from different organs, associations, and groups that unambiguously demand a basic attitude different from the official Church. In particular the "Announcement of Disappointed Feelings and Hopes," which was provoked most recently by the official Church, is surely "an opportunity for responsible and critical commitment to the Church" and not just on the part of the Swiss Union for the Concerns of Council and Synod: "In the future this commitment to the Church might be used for the tasks of the Church in the world. For that the Church's leaders must seriously involve themselves in the situation of Christians who have to prove their faith in different areas (e.g., pastoral care, education, politics, culture)."

A Church of renovation and innovation — this means for *the Church of the future* (see the declaration of the young persons' ministry of the Union of Catholic Youth in the diocese of Rottenburg-Stuttgart):

- A Church that exposes itself to the gospel and thus experiences and makes visible Christ as the measure and foundation.
- A Church that is not an end in itself, but a way to Christ, a sacrament, a sign of salvation for the salvation of our world.
- A Church in which human limitation, guilt, and sin are not passed over in silence, but are understood as an expression of its being on the way.
- A Church that knows itself as God's wandering people, which must always renew and reform itself.
- A Church that is aware of the support of the Spirit of God, that is rich through the multiplicity of lived faith and hence can calmly and trustingly endure opposition and allow experimentation.
- A Church as a place of brotherliness where Christians share things — including their faith — where they learn to bear and endure one another, where there can be conflict and there must be reconciliation.
- A Church in which prejudices are disassembled and conflicts are settled fairly, where the principles of life are not dominion and power but nonviolence and service.

If we wished to concretize somewhat these fundamental demands of the gospel for the current situation of the Church in West Germany, on the basis of the voices, now loud and clear, from the Church itself, we would have to think particularly of the Church's work with young people, religious instruction, pastoral care, theology, the magisterium, and the position of the Church in society. Here I must renounce making such suggestions but I point to the impressive positions taken by the most diverse authorities and groups in the documentation mentioned.

To many people what has taken place in our Church over the last months has seemed like a spectral farce. Catholics claw and tear one another in the struggle for orthodoxy, religious formulas, and infallibility, while the world around them threatens to go to pieces. This blindness to reality is itself the greatest expression of the crisis of the Church that we currently find ourselves in. We are no longer aware of what is really going on in the world. But that is the whole point:

- In a world that has become increasingly cold, brutal, and uninhabitable;

49

- where resources are in increasingly short supply and the battles over their distribution are increasingly harsh;
- where the great political and theological systems oppose one another in an increasingly less conciliatory and more saber-rattling mode;
- where mutual mistrust grows and the arms race continues to heat up; in a world where the relation between the rulers and the ruled, the powerful and the powerless, the rich and the poor, is becoming increasingly inhuman, where the balance between technology and humanity, economy and ecology is ever more difficult to establish, because conditions do not permit it.

Here, I think, Christians have in fact a decisive, indispensable contribution to make for the promotion of the welfare of humanity. For these far more complex social questions Catholic Christians await ongoing suggestive answers from, among others, the Church's leadership. They would be glad to get some constructive help here.

In conclusion I quote once again the federal leadership of the Catholic Youth Community:

The call for unity, so that the Church can make its contribution in today's world, was answered in a way that we consider false: By the call to believe, to overcome the dangers of the age through inner discipline. When Jesus says to his friends, "Those who wish to keep their life will lose it and are already losing it, but those who commit their life and give it away will gain it and are already gaining it" (after John 12:25), this holds just as well for his Church. We do not want a Church for its own sake; we want a Church that is a "sign of the unity of human beings with God and of human beings with one another" (Cardinal Döpfner).

The way of Jesus, the way of freedom that he took, was not to demand dogmas and laws. It was the challenge: Change yourselves (continually), have the courage to be free and to take over the responsibility for your life and the life of your fellow human beings. God is with you. Jesus has already shown by example what such a life in responsible freedom consistently means. Even if we don't live up to this claim placed on us, we have no choice but to apply it as the criterion for our actions and those of the whole Church.

That is what we strive and struggle for. Despite everything we do not give up, we do not resign. Those of us below do not hand the

Church over to those who are above: All of us together are the Church. And for the future of this Church in all our work, thought, struggles, and prayers we trust in him who alone is the true Lord of the Church.

6

Church from Above —
Church from Below

Considerations on a Charismatic Structure for the Church

The expression "from below" has very quickly gained popularity (especially in German-speaking countries) in theology and in the Church at large, first in christology, then in ecclesiology. Yet this term must not be used uncritically: it is useful only inasmuch as it helps to clarify that picture. The discussion is not about words — what matters is the situation itself.

A few years ago, not unconnected with discussions about the papacy and infallibility, about twenty very distinguished groups in Germany (including some parishes) met to organize a so-called *Katholikentag von unten*, a kind of grassroots national pastoral congress, to run parallel to the one held every two years by the hierarchy and associated lay extensions.

This "Congress from Below," held in Berlin in June 1980, surprised even its originators with its success. It gained the attention of the official *Katholikentag* and of the general public. It did not seek confrontation with the institutional Church, the "Church from Above," but did not hesitate to speak the truth about the Church as it was seen and voice its concern about the position of the Church in modern society.

Taboos such as human rights, celibacy, homosexuality, etc. were taken up and open wounds in hierarchical practice pointed out. Literally thousands from the official *Katholikentag* came to the meetings.

Ed. Note: This first part is a summary of the original German article. The remaining parts, beginning with "Strategic Guidelines for a Basic Church, on p. 55, have been translated in full.

In September 1980 representatives of the same groups and networks met again and resolved to resume the impulses emerging from the *Katholikentag von unten* and to form the *Initiative Kirche von unten*. It called itself an "Initiative by the Church from below" in order to indicate that it did not see itself as an alternative Church but as loyal opposition from within, campaigning for objectives such as the following:

- to achieve more openness, pluralism, and tolerance within the Church;
- to maintain the impulses of the Second Vatican Council and of the Synod of German Bishops in Würzburg;
- to uphold the necessity of a real socio-political engagement of Christians and Churches;
- to bring to fruition, in parishes all over West Germany, the impulses of the "Poor Church" of the Third World and its basic communities.

Within the framework of a new and different Christian lifestyle it has two aims:

- not the seizure of power within the Church, but the dismantling of the current power structure or at least containing and restricting the power of the ruling ecclesiastical bureaucracy;
- not being an alternative Church, but a new and different model of the Church with a greater orientation to basic Christian and democratic principles of freedom, equality, and brother/sisterhood.

Thus came to light within the Church of West Germany another Church of laity, theologians, and pastors.

Originally the Church called by God through Jesus Christ — one might say "from above" in a different sense — saw itself basically and as a whole a Church from below because all of us are "the people of God." The primitive Church knew that it was God's people: ecclesia-assembly-community of the faithful. In the understanding of the New Testament it is impossible to separate the Church from the laity.

The clerical or hierarchical misunderstanding of the Church is to identify it directly or indirectly with the clergy or even the hierarchy. In the New Testament the word *laos* signifies no distinction within the community between those "ordained" and "not ordained." The distinction is made not within the community of Christians but between it and the pagan world. The people of God were *laos*, the pagan was a *laikos*, a "layperson."

Undoubtedly, there are distinctions within the New Testament people of God relating to different services, functions, gifts, and duties. But they are not described in terms of *laos* or *laikos*. On the contrary, all these distinctions are of secondary importance as compared with the absolutely fundamental equality of all God's people.

These original communities were solidarity groups in which, according to Paul, each person had his or her charisma, gifts with which to build and sustain the community. Hence one can speak, in this sense, of a charismatic structure of the Church, not a uniform but a pluriform Church with a multitude of gifts in individuals and groups.

How then could such a Church with so much freedom preserve order? According to Paul it is God's Spirit who is the prime mover in creating order. Unity and order are not established by disciplining or levelling the variety within the Church. No, it is particularly beneficial for unity and order that everyone has his or her charisma. So the first rule of a charismatic Church structure is as follows: everyone has gifts but they are not the same and anybody who takes away the exercise of these gifts creates disorder, not order and unity. These gifts, however, are not for the person himself or herself. They are not to rule over others, but to serve them. There is no charisma of being a Prince of the Church or a Lord Spiritual. This then is the second rule for a charismatic church order: not domination or confrontation, but togetherness and living for one another. Hence Paul's vision of love as the first fruit of the Spirit and the highest of all charisms. The third rule is that of subordination to Christ, "unio" with the Lord, and thus "com-unio," the community of the brothers and sisters in Jesus. Communion, not domination, certainly no subordination to levels of authority created by the world.

Finally, all of us are the one Church of Christ which is in its essence a Church from below. Church from below is not something new; it is the essence of the New Testament Church. There is no place for a Church between heaven and earth which could put itself in any official capacity in God's place and above the people, dictators over our faith instead of fellow-workers for our happiness (2 Cor. 1:24).

We all must start from below. "From the depths I cry to you, Lord" (Ps. 130:1). The greatest among us must be like the youngest and the leader must be like the servant (Luke 22:25ff.). This must be the biblical basis of any ecclesiology which must never degenerate into a hierarchology.

In essence, all of us in the Church are "from below." Only Christ is "from above," as John points out clearly in 8:23. So if any, however pious, make themselves God's representatives and exalt themselves above others so that people kneel before them, such persons had better beware. There is only one who is greater than others, the one who humbled himself to "accepting death, death on a cross" and therefore was raised high by God above all others (Phil. 2:8–11).

Only Jesus rules in his Church. This may sound essentially Protestant but is also essentially Catholic. We say it every time we recite the Gloria, "You alone are the Lord."

Strategic Guidelines for a Basic Church

These are then some of the biblical impulses and motives behind the *epoch-making changes effected by the Second Vatican Council* in its teaching and its practical aspects. It soon became clear how much explosive power continues to reside in its use of biblical language:

- The Church understood not as hierarchy, but as people of God. (The relevant chapter in the Constitution on the Church was given precedence over that on the hierarchy.)
- The Church interpreted not simply as warning and exhorting others, but seen as a sinning community in need of repeated reformation (*ecclesia semper reformanda*).
- The Church understood not as a sort of sacral world organization, but as a local Church in which every individual can make his or her contribution according to each person's charisma.
- Offices in the Church understood not as holy domination, but as service to its people.
- The pope not as spiritual autocrat and object of a personality cult, but as a colleague within the College of Bishops, as servant of God's servants.
- Hence the Church as community in solidarity, in brotherhood and sisterhood, not celebrating itself triumphalistically but self-critically correcting its own mistakes and concentrating on its great task in modern society.

In short: a Church such as was presented by Pope John XXIII — as opposed to the Pius popes — and was articulated by the Council and Pope Paul albeit with many concessions to the still mighty curia. At all events, it was still possible to have the welcome reform of the liturgy (in the vernacular), to form parish and diocesan councils, to enable ecumenical co-operation at the local levels such as one sees nowadays in all such places where the parish priest himself cooperates and initiates with sincerity.

But "from above" all this looked very different from the way it was seen from below. All those essentially biblical impulses and motives were in the postconciliar period increasingly constricted into narrow channels by pope, curia, and finally by the bishops. And if they could not be controlled in such a way there came the disciplining. It reminds one of the Roman policy after the Ecumenical Council of Constance or the century before the Reformation! The Church's rulers, those "from above," saw Vatican II as the furthest limit of the Church's changes and reforms. "From below," however, it was seen simply as a first step toward "razing the walls of the fortifications completely to the ground" as Hans Urs von Balthasar put it so poignantly in 1952. There grew then a frightening *discrepancy between the promises of the Council and their post-conciliar fulfillment* which is felt all the more strongly today precisely because hopes were raised and expectations aroused.

Indeed there were at the beginning of the 1970s, especially in German-speaking countries, *synods* planned and organized with much idealism and great pomp. And during such synods many voices from below were at first heard. But because of the obstructiveness of the curia and some bishops too amenable to the curia's wishes many important questions were never discussed. Or if it came to a discussion or consultation no decisions were made. Or decisions reached were never confirmed by the bishops or the pope. Thus the abolition of matrimonial impediment of denominational difference, the admission of those who have divorced and remarried to the sacraments, the ordination of married men, etc. were indeed sought by the synods but given short shrift by those in power without any serious protestations. There followed polarization and the internal emigration often of the very best.

In this disappointing situation it is therefore not surprising that under the present pontiff many thinking Christians are becoming more and more convinced that an initiative from below is necessary, that the model of the Church from below must be understood afresh and brought into realization. These now critical Christians share the conviction that:

- we cannot expect in our country — as distinct from Latin America — any initiative "from above" in the near future which would make the Church here more free, more democratic, more Christian in doctrine and life;

- the individual can achieve little working from below for a truly new order in Church and society;

- more and more *pluriform, autonomous, self-contained Christian groups,* as much as possible *independent* of the conservative hierarchy, must be fostered or where necessary founded, groups which *must work "from below."* These will not be new Churches or sects but movements within the existing Church which is so bitterly in need of a much more comprehensive reform. We need something like an ecclesiastical task force of mature Christians who have outgrown the status of "Father's children" and want to be taken seriously by those in power, sooner rather than later. "Solidarity" could become their watchword as it was and is with the Polish trade union movement from below.

The Basic Movement

Such *basic groupings*, which try to live their Christian faith in a new form and to realize it in terms of contemporary life, exist already in great numbers and diversity. I should like to essay at least a thumbnail sketch of the basic movement.

There are, first, the *basic communities* or *basic churches*, which may or may not be identical with a local church or parish. They rightly bear the name of community or church *if* they constitute a regular worshipping community (= ecclesia) — if in them the gospel is proclaimed, the eucharistic meal in memory of Jesus Christ is held, new members are received through baptism in his name, and both within and without the Church the gospel is made effective.

But besides the basic communities in the strict sense, there are, second, a large number of other *basic groups*: personal communities, action- or task-orientated groups, spontaneous groups, solidarity groups, initiatives. . . . For example, groups of Christians strive in the spirit of Vatican II and later synods:

- for an open, searching, and listening Church, for democratic and partnership structures or
- for new forms in the liturgy and the sacrament of reconciliation;
- for human rights in the Church, for an acknowledgement of the full value of the "layperson," equal rights for women, the ordination of women;
- for a new understanding of the "priest" as a spiritual leader of the community and for the abolition of compulsory celibacy;
- for real ecumenical dialogue in theory and practice;
- for a better understanding of homosexuals and other minorities in society;
- for human rights and political prisoners in countries such as Chile, South Africa, or the Soviet Union or for the poor and oppressed in this or that country.

All of them — women and men, theologians and nontheologians, academics and workers, young and old — try in their special way to find and realize what is *contained in the Christian message*, explicitly or implicitly, *as that which liberates* in order to make it effective as critical potential for our own individual or social situation.

Many know already that countries like West Germany are not, as is often thought, somehow underdeveloped countries with regard to basic groups. It must however be acknowledged that this movement from below is much more extensive in the Netherlands, Italy, Spain, and France, but also in the United States and in Latin America. And at the same time the consciousness is growing everywhere that the different groups in all their justified individuality must in no way isolate themselves, but that *maximum contact with each other* is of utmost importance: on both national and international levels.

The founding of the German "Initiative of the Church from Below" and also the numerous international contacts between the different basic movements are to be seen in this context. In all this the conviction has arisen that the "activists" and the "thinkers" must work together and — as has occurred in various instances — should support each other in difficulties. In this, public opinion often comes to their aid, insofar as it is interested in a more open, compassionate, and humane Church: against all repression by the hierarchy the media often give to those movements the necessary space in which to proclaim the truth as they see it, so that those movements may become effective in society and within the Church.

Especially in view of the pope's constant visits to different countries where he is systematically sheltered from critical questions and accompanied throughout by pious TV commentators, one must not forget the real situation: in controversial ecclesiastical matters, *pope and bishops have only a minority on their side* whereas *the Church from below has the overwhelming majority* on its side. Contrary to the doctrine of the Church from Above — a doctrine which it promotes with all available means, i.e., that it embodies the "complete truth of the Catholic Faith" — it remains a fact that for example in West Germany:

56 percent of all Catholics are against papal infallibility;
57 percent for the ordination of women;
67 percent for joint services of Catholics and Protestants;
71 percent for a remarriage in church of divorced persons;
72 percent for priests marrying;
73 percent for abortion under specific circumstances;
74 percent for abolition of impediments to "mixed marriage";
81 percent for permitting contraception.

When we consider the age-pyramid, we see that we shall soon have to speak of the bishops as generals without armies. Were all those who — in the words of the Congregation for the Doctrine of the Faith, December 18, 1979, about a certain theologian — "depart from the complete truth of the Catholic faith," no longer to pay the church tax (which is compulsory in West Germany), the whole apparatus of this, the most bureaucratized Church in the world, would at once collapse.

But let us leave this point. The discussion on the basis, the purpose, the functions, and the methods of the basic movement is, in any case, in full swing.

To clarify this discussion we shall now develop some strategical guidelines on the basis of our theological premises, guidelines which shall not deal particularly with this or that point but more with the general direction of the argument. This developing "Church from Below" is to be theologically legitimated in its actuality, its independence, and indeed its churchliness — as shown — but at the same time it must be kept from sliding into a ghetto or sect situation.

There are two aspects on which most would nowadays agree: Firstly, that the Latin American basic communities cannot, without further ado, be subsumed into the landscape of highly industrialized countries of the West such as West Germany. The basis of our communities is, after all, not a poor, underprivileged majority of the population lacking literacy, industrial organization, fulfillment of basic needs, and protection and support in the pursuit of fundamental political and social requirements. Our communities here live in totally different circumstances and in relative prosperity. As a spokesman for the AGP, the West German Priests and Solidarity Group, said recently, "Imitations of successes abroad will not work for us. We must look closely at where, in our situation, we can find resources for a Church that is open to the future and which has a humane concern. In West Germany, we must find our own way."

Secondly, our Church from Below receives strong impulses from the Latin American basic communities in many ways, making us aware of our special social situation, so that we can leave behind the "Guardian Church" and the "Servicing Church" (J. B. Metz) and take upon us more decisively our own responsibility for ourselves as Christians and as Church.

The theologian Hermann Pius Siller who works in a basic community in Frankfurt comments as follows on the sentence "we must find our own way" (replying, incidentally, to earlier remarks by Fr. Klusmann):

Speaking of "our way" is to refer in its theological context to the congregation as community (*koinonia*) of autonomous members, a community such as we are by nature not yet, but wish to become. The expression "our own way" refers to the specific situation of the community, independently of central control. Expressions like "our own search" or that we want to find "our own way" simply refer to the refusal of the congregation to be merely consumers of what is dealt out by the ecclesiastical administration.

In short: *No imitation* of Latin America models, *but inspiration* by such models. This is clearly and positively expressed in one of the books by Leonardo Boff, the Brazilian priest whose views on liberation theology have been subject to the Vatican's scrutiny, where he deals with basic communities in Latin America. It is also explained in one of Norbert Greinacher's books on the Church of the Poor and the theology of liberation.

But here we run up against one of the major problems as discussed at present within the Church. Where should basic groups and basic communities be — *within or outside the existing geographical parishes?*

In part this problem is no longer quite so acute in that geographical boundaries have become somewhat irrelevant for many because of present-day mobility. Many worshippers in our towns come from other parishes. Territorially defined parishes are gradually becoming "gathered" parishes. And when enlightened parish priests succeed in activating such parishes by real communication through the liturgy, there too basic initiatives are developed. In such circumstances the question of "inside or outside" or even against the parish solves itself for the most part. Groups and networks "from below" but at peace with the parish are possible, either within the framework of the parish itself or loosely connected with it.

Our *parishes* (now pastoral and administrative units of the institutional Church) must become real *communities* (gatherings of fully responsible members) as is sought by the Tübingen scholar and yet very practical theologian Norbert Greinacher, and as is understood by many parish priests.

One has to agree with Pastor Ferdinand Kerstiens, one of the leading members of the West German Priests and Solidarity Groups, when he pleads for the possibility of critical group and community work within the traditional parishes, work to be carried out in smaller units on the basis of a *pluralism within the Church.* He said,

It would be pastorally much better to have many centers, many points of crystallization, where smaller units of diverse structure and motivation can gather, so that as many people as possible may find a possibility of identification in the Church.... What matters is ... breaking up the mono-structure of a parish, the one-sidedly religious or political stance which is perhaps right for some people in a parish but not for the whole of the community as it excludes others. It can therefore be dangerous to regard the parish as one large unit. For then in practice this unity is determined by one small group. It serves the community better when the parish is understood as a dynamic coming-together of diverse substructures. This pluralism is grounded theologically in the notion of diverse charisms, no single one of which can claim to be solely decisive.

But how can such a new group come about in an established parish? In order to achieve more plurality, so says Kerstiens, a "pastoral practice of limited conflict" is needed. When there is controversy, new and other groups within the community could have their say without leaving the field to the grouping which alone has the say in practice. Parish priests and other leaders of the parish would have to take part in such discussions, not as leaders but as equal partners. This critical approach should aim at the other person's becoming a co-agent, a partner, not the object of my pastoral effort: the renewal we seek must become reality *through the people*.

Basic Church and Institutional Church

We can therefore conclude:

- Basic Christian groups are not in principle against authority but they expect such authority to be based on the gospel and not just on canon law or the traditional practices of the community establishment.

- Basic Christian groups are not in principle against church institutions but they do expect the institutions to let them have the necessary freedom to fulfil themselves and the special task they have been given.

- Basic Christian groups want to remain in the Church but they expect the institutional Church to be flexible enough at least to tolerate them even if it feels incapable of promoting them.

Thus *it depends largely on the institutional Church* and especially on the bishops whether the basic groups develop within the official Church and become fruitful there or whether they develop on the margin of the Church or even outside and against it. Here are two contrasting examples:

In *Italy*, the Roman curia and the episcopate largely reject the basic groups and seek to suppress them; thus they push them into opposition to the institutional Church. It is questionable whether in the long run the hierarchy will maintain the upper hand. Where bishops and parish priests reject all the concerns of the Church from Below, then as an emergency solution, a basic group or even a basic community outside the geographically or territorially defined parish or official community can certainly be a legitimate possibility.

In *Latin America* the bishops welcome and support basic groups, as is expressed in the documents of Medellín and Puebla; therefore the groups develop within the official Church and become more and more its main base. There also one encounters fewer problems with young people and women leaving the Church. In *Spain,* where according to the latest accounts from the bishops eleven hundred Catholic basic groups exist, two-thirds of these maintain a close connection with the parish. Now the bishops there want to establish a "network of basic groups" and have sought the groups' assistance in this.

It is thoroughly desirable that *every basic community,* although not necessarily every basic group, *should have its ordained community leader* preside at its eucharistic celebration. Whether a basic community can exist without a community leader and validly celebrate the Eucharist is a matter of controversy among theologians as well as among the basic communities themselves.

A much broader view of the situation is therefore recommended: "from below" and "from above" must not be seen as necessarily opposing forces. Even the holder of church office, whether parish priest, bishop, or pope, does not have to be a kind of commander-in-chief, but can in his whole administration be at one in feeling, thought, and action with the people "below" at grassroots. If he does this, then — whatever his official position — he belongs of course to the Church from Below, and not to the Church from Above. A final question:

What Are the Ecumenical Implications of a Church from Below?

1. It is ecumenically important and quite in keeping with the mind of the Reformed Churches and the Eastern Church that the Church not be understood from above as an Official Church, but be seen afresh from below as a community of believers, as the people of God, a movement of the Spirit, the following of Jesus Christ.

2. It is ecumenically important and quite in keeping with the mind of the Reformed Churches too that office in the Church be thought of not as hierarchy, as holy dominion, but as *diakonia,* as selfless service.

3. There is ecumenical importance and solid Gospel thinking in the key Catholic concept of a basic Church (initiative Church, community Church), where the ruling principles are freedom, partnership, collegiality, solidarity, brotherhood and sisterhood; where there is more convincing than commanding, more doing than preaching, more help-

ful dealing with one another than bureaucratic-autocratic proceeding against others; where, in short, an alternative Christian praxis is the order of the day.

In other words, it is important that between God and humanity, between God and the Church, the Above and Below — the infinite difference despite all immanence — *should* be stressed. But in the Church itself the Above and Below should be replaced by a Being With. Our task is to work for a Church of the people, in which people are no longer the object of patronizing treatment but the subject of their own history before God.

7

Longing for John XXIV:
In Memory of Pope John XXIII

If John XXIV had been sitting in the chair of St. Peter for the past ten years, we would scarcely have any strong memories of Pope Giovanni: At best we would recall him as an inspirer and initiator of the Council, at most as a forerunner in the process of renewal in the Catholic Church that lasted a good twenty-five years but that was now fully unfolded. We would remember him as the man who, in line with the will of many cardinals who elected him then as a seventy-seven-year-old compromise candidate, was originally supposed to be a transitional pope.

No Transfiguration

But for the past ten years the man sitting on the papal throne — and who can overlook the fact? — has been Pius XIII. And so at once John XXIII is no longer a mere precursor in our memory. No, he instantly becomes for us the great contrasting figure, the counterpole, the decisive alternative for a different, for a more human, more Christian, ecumenical pontificate.

Now the last thing that Angelo Roncalli, the winegrower's son, would have wanted was his transfiguration: being idealized and made into a hero, or even a saint. And remembering him should not lead to such exaggeration — even when the current Roman regime, cutting a swath from Holland across Austria even into Switzerland, still systematically and unscrupulously disdains the will of the Catholic people and clergy by appointing conformist bishops, as is customary only in "people's democracies" and military dictatorships. John XXIII too showed weaknesses, made mistakes, had his limitations. He too never really became master of his own Roman power structure, ruled at cross purposes with it; and the Second Vatican Council had to pay for this with countless compromises and defects.

Pope John in no way saw himself as an epoch-making figure, and yet his papacy marked an epoch. He was no restorer, but an inaugurator: a renewer of the Church. He didn't need an autocratic style or repressive measures against bishops, theologians, and nuns in order to lead the world Church. He was satisfied with an unpretentious style of little, successful gestures, symbolic actions, and Christian signs, in order to win the hearts of men and women and to change the Church.

He did not wish to teach from the top down and to force discipline through censorship. On the contrary, working from a deep understanding for the successes and needs of the modern world, he wanted to help as a brother, as we heard everywhere in all his statements, last of all in the encyclical *Pacem in terris*, with its advocacy of peace and justice, religious freedom, human rights, and the brotherhood and sisterhood of all.

Pope John XXIII did not need some thirty-six trips around the world, consuming millions and millions of dollars, in order to get a hearing from the world Church. And yet people all over the world heard his voice far beyond the limits of the Church, indeed beyond Christendom, because his words, inspired by the gospel, spoke immediately to their hearts. He didn't need television and media spectaculars to get a hearing in the Church. He did not like his picture taken in pious poses; he joked about how unphotogenic he was. And yet the pictures of him were attractive, often moving: that guileless, humble, kind, in short, lovable face. No, this pope was surely no "great communicator," nor a great diplomat, linguist, jurist, or learned theologian.

Nevertheless precisely because he was not all that, he was loved by the people. If you ask a taxi driver in Rome today what the Romans think of the present pope, you can get the answer: *"il Papa dei Romani è papa Giovanni."* "The pope of the Romans is Pope John." The next pope, they hope, will again be one of them....

Surprising Results

People in fact have not forgotten all the many little anecdotes circulating about him. Their point generally consists in the way that something surprising, overwhelming, unexpected went out from this pope. He was a pope who broke away from the script: here a bit of irony and liberating humor at his own expense, there a piece of renunciation of power and self-abasement. Here a a gesture to overcome separations and fill in gaps, there a sign of reconciliation and fraternity. "I am Joseph, your brother," he said to Jewish visitors, stepped down from his throne and sat among them on a chair. He was the first pope to give up the *sedia gestatoria* and a lot of the "pomp and circumstance." To avoid applause he had the Apostles' Creed sung when he entered St. Peter's.

Quite spontaneously, without making publicity and a ritual out of it, he personally visited poor people, comforted the sick in hospitals, sought out priests who had suffered shipwreck in their lives. Indeed he once visited thieves and murderers in the Roman state prison, and on this occasion he did not deliver a programmatic (and ghostwritten) speech, but simply and comfortingly told about his uncle, who had been imprisoned for poaching.

Truly, John XXIII was a pope who often slipped out of the papal role and had the unique capacity, which is available only to the true Christian, to relativize himself, his person, and his office. Nor have people forgotten the anecdote about the conversation with a care-worn bishop: If he, Giovanni, was so troubled that he couldn't sleep, he would have "the pope" say to him: "Angelo, don't take yourself so seriously."

No wonder that this pope, more than any of his predecessors, had a magnetic effect on contemporary artists, both sculptors and writers, as Karl-Josef Kuschel has shown in his fine book entitled *Stellvertreter Christi? Der Papst in der zeitgenössischen Literatur* (1980; Christ's deputy: The pope in contemporary literature):

> Marie Louise Kaschnitz called him a "man disguised as pope," the Brazilian playwright João Bethencourt dedicated a play to him, *The Day the Pope Was Kidnapped*; Wolfgang Hildesheimer wrote "Exercises" featuring him; the Italian sculptor Giacomo Manzu did bronze busts of him and, full of admiration and reverence, had his personal memories of him written up. And in his novel *The Clown*, Heinrich Böll has his "hero" on the staircase of the central train station in Bonn softly intone the song of "Poor Pope John," full of resignation and melancholy, on the guitar. Indeed Böll's Clown can identify with this pope, because John too is one of the phantasts and dreamers, the innocent and pure, who can fall between the millstones of the system, one of those foolish fighters for a better Church in a better world, whose power is their innocence and whose weapon is their love of people: "I resolved to travel to Rome and also to ask the pope for an audience. He too had a little of the wise old clown about him, and after all the figure of the harlequin was created in Bergamo."

The Epochal Achievement

As unforgettable as his person was, what he achieved for the Catholic Church was unforgettable too. In five years he renewed the Catholic

Church more than his predecessors had in five hundred years. Only now can we get a more precise overview of the historical connections. John was the pope who undertook the challenge of catching up at once with *two epochal paradigm changes* for the Catholic Church: the duplication of the Reformation-Protestant paradigm change as well as the Enlightenment-modern paradigm. Only with John did the Middle Ages come to an end in the Catholic Church: Both the Counter-Reformation of the sixteenth and seventeenth centuries and the antimodernism of the eighteenth and nineteenth centuries had tried to conserve by any means the medieval structures in doctrine, liturgy, and discipline. Without John XXIII there would have been no Vatican II, no comprehensive renewal of the Church, no popular liturgy, no ecumenical opening, no liberating commitment of the Catholic Church in today's society.

More concretely, Angelo Roncalli, a youthful friend of the Italian "modernist" Ernesto Buonaiuti and accused by curial reactionaries as the pope of "modernism," called back to the Council the theologians unjustly condemned under Pius XII, and he reintegrated them into the process of the renewal of Catholic liturgy and the Church. He invited to the Council the followers of Martin Luther, Zwingli, and Calvin as well as the representatives of other churches, and thereby made ecumenism the concern not just of a few specialists but of the whole Catholic Church.

He removed from the liturgy discriminatory texts on the Jews, opened the Catholic Church to the Jews, and awakened in it a sensitivity toward Islam. He made possible a phase of dialogue with the world religions derived from India and China and relieved the Catholic Church's anxiety over the encounter with non-Catholics, non-Christians, and atheists. He put an end to all verbal anticommunism, and was the first pope to speak up decisively for the observance of human rights, which had been solemnly condemned by the popes of previous centuries. Without John there would have been no taking down of the fortress mentality that the Catholic Church was trapped in. Without him there would have been no demolition of the bastions behind which the Catholic Church had withdrawn; without him there would be no mass in the vernacular, no common worship with the Orthodox and Protestants, no opening toward the Communist East, no flinging open of windows, no liberating renovation of tradition, no comprehensive new evangelization and new Christianization of a sclerotic institution.

What was behind all this? An ambitious plan to make Church history? The calculations of a pontifical strategy that sought to increase power by an embrace? No, astonishing as it is, John XXIII conceived the plan of the Council from the simple, childlike conviction of the believing Christian who is persuaded that with God's help something serious must be done to overcome the misery of the church schism and rigidity in the Church.

He called the Council as a man of God who refused be to be frightened by the risks of such an undertaking and by the prophets of doom around him, but let himself be borne up by a holy "optimism." This was nothing else but Christian hope as unconquerable as it was realistic. He knew of the danger that his plan for the Council might be thwarted by the forces in his immediate environment. But, *"Il Concilio si deve fare malgrado la curia,"* The Council must be carried out despite the curia, as he had once said to some pastors from his native province of Bergamo, who were surprised that not everybody in Rome thought like the pope himself.

Here he proceeded carefully and prudently. He was helped by a completely unsentimental Christian love that guided him in his daily work. That was the source of his aversion to harsh condemnations, to ruthless anathemas and excommunications, to unjust inquisitorial procedures. He never hurt anyone, he never refused to engage in dialogue, even with the critics in his own Church. He often got what he wanted very unobtrusively and in apparently roundabout ways: "Pope Giovanni reaches his goal the way water does," one of his friends told me. For a while he allowed the ecumenical goal of the Council to be passed over in silence by his co-workers. But when a visitor complained about this, he answered, "I'll retrieve it." And then he founded the Secretariat for Promoting Christian Unity, an important prerequisite for the success of the Council, especially since he appointed as head of this secretariat Cardinal Bea, who even in difficult matters always had the full confidence of the pope and always gave him his own.

John XXIII was a rather intuitive pragmatist, but it was just this that helped the Council and ecumenical efforts. This pope had no time for the doctrinaire approach that because of its Pharisaic self-righteousness, its impatience, and its lack of understanding for the genuine concerns of others is the greatest and most dangerous enemy of all innovative and ecumenical strivings. This was the actual reason why he ordered the theological preparatory commission for the Council to prepare no new dogmas. Pope John XXIII was convinced that in today's situation humanity would be helped not by the repetition or definition of old truths but through a timely proclamation of the gospel that makes use of new forms of expression and knows how to distinguish between the substance and the wording of the old doctrine. John XXIII stated this with extraordinary impressiveness in his address opening the Council, which decisively shaped the course of the Council's transactions.

No, John XXIII was not bent on going down in history as a pope who, like Pius IX and Pius XII, defined a new dogma, about Mary no less, without having been challenged by heresy. "I am not infallible," he once said in a conversation with Greek seminarians. And when they looked at him in amazement, he had to add, with a smile, "I am not infallible. The pope is infallible only when he speaks *ex cathedra*. But I will never speak *ex cathedra*." And in fact he never did. Collegiality with the bishops was not a decorative frill of authoritarianism for him, but — although it had not yet been solemnly proclaimed by the Council — a natural conviction.

The Legacy

Pope John XXIII's program was not to make a triumphal exhibition of Roman Catholicism all over the world in beautiful (but ineffectual) words and gestures with the help of the mass media. He had no time for showy productions. His program — which these days is once again greatly despised — was energetically to renew the Catholic Church itself by the spirit of the gospel, and thus to prepare the reunion of separated Christians. Instead of the ideology of a Roman Catholicism, Rome and the Catholic Church should now be on the way to a comprehensive Christian ecumene.

We can gather what the pope's whole position was: Had he not died right after the first session, he would surely have had the Council discuss in all freedom disputed issues such as birth control, celibacy, mixed marriage, divorces, intercommunion, and reform of the papacy. His successor, however, violated all collegiality and took over these controversial questions for himself. In this way he managed to reach the wrong decision on them after the Council — under renewed pressure from the uneducable citizens of the papal state. The years 1967 and 1968, when the encyclicals on celibacy and birth control were issued, gave the first clear signs of a reactionary turn. We can imagine what would have happened if the Second Vatican Council had been allowed to decide these issues itself, along with other disputed questions (religious freedom, attitude toward the Jews, the vernacular in the liturgy, Marianism, etc.), in keeping with the great tradition of ecumenical Councils: What enormous losses the Catholic Church would have been spared in the postconciliar period — from the exodus of countless priests, religious, and laypeople to the silent departure of couples in mixed marriages and remarried divorced people. In Pope John's times we did not have all the unnecessary and damaging tensions and polarizations in the Catholic Church that resulted from the curia's attempts at braking and blocking.

But despite all the failures and compromises during the Council, despite all the failures by the bishops who have once again become intimidated, and despite the whole present-day violent blockade of internal church renewal, of veiled obstruction of every ecumenical understanding, and the hindering of constructive solutions from Roman headquarters, the problems are, as everyone knows, not disappearing just because they are denied. They remain, they accumulate, become ever more pressing and one day will break through. One need think only of the appointment of reactionary bishops everywhere in the world and of the worldwide, continually intensifying catastrophic lack of priests. All this must be laid at the door of the pope from Poland with his intransigence and inability to learn from history.

Sad as this is, the spiritual "balance of payments deficit" has grown astronomically over the last few years. The Vatican has tried to master the profound crisis with outdated formulas. What this boils down to is that nothing truly innovative has been done in the last ten years to handle the true emergencies of the Church. Then there were the unexplained scandals in the Vatican's finances. Morality was mostly preached to others. Secret organizations like Opus Dei are allowed to carry on their dirty business.... John Paul II's successor will have his work cut out for him.

It is only to be regretted that the popes do not, like American presidents and many pastors in Switzerland, have to be re-elected by the people from time to time. But in any case the Council has already laid down a binding retirement age of seventy-five for bishops. Why shouldn't it also be applicable to the bishop of Rome? Don't the arguments also, and especially, hold good for him?

However the development on particular matters may have been, the Catholic Church can no longer move back behind John XXIII. With him a new epoch of church history began, an epoch of new vitality, new freedom, and new hope. And this cannot be suppressed by Pope Wojtyla, who remains trapped in the medieval–Counter-Reformation–antimodern paradigm of his homeland. Pope John stands for this new *hope:* his personal style, his individual radiance, his achievement for the renewal of the Catholic Church, his efforts for the ecumene.

We who will soon be able to look back on the whole twentieth century may rightly say: *The greatest pope of this century is Pope John XXIII.* He is the true renewer of the Church and the first ecumenical pope. In a brief five years he became and has remained to this day a uniquely integrative figure for all humanity, mourned by Christians and Jews, atheists and the heterodox, when he succumbed to stomach cancer on June 3, 1963.

But greatness? Is greatness even a category for Christians? If one wishes to sense the last *mystery of his greatness,* one will have to say: This pope was great, not because he wanted to be a great lord, but because he wanted to be the servant of all: "servants of the servants of God" (Pope Gregory the Great). Servant of his fellow bishops and priests, of Christians and non-Christians, men and women. Here he had the word of Another behind him, one who makes his greatness unassailable: "Whoever among you wants to be the greatest let him be your servant." That is how he tried to shape this Petrine *service*, based on the gospel, in the Church once more in a new evangelical fashion, following the demands of the gospel: "You, strengthen your brothers!" And precisely because he brought the primal element of the gospel again to the light, he met with sympathy from many Protestants. For this reason his pontificate was more human, more Christian, more ecumenical. And for this reason he is the greatest pope of our century. Do we need to come up with any more reasons why today more than ever we long for John XXIV?

Part Three —

Solving
Problems

On the Way to a New Church Order: A Theological Case for Shared Decision-Making by the Laity

A Blind Spot in the Decree on the Laity

The theme to be treated here is, surprisingly, not to be found in the Vatican II Decree on the Apostolate of the Laity. That fact makes the matter difficult. Participation, cooperation, collaboration of the laity in the decisions of the Church? People like to talk of the participation of the laity in the *life* (not the decisions) of the Church. They also like to speak of the participation of the laity in the decisions of the *world* (but not of the Church). They do not at all like to speak, at least in official binding documents, of the participation of the laity in the *decisions* of the *Church*. Nevertheless it is precisely here that the question of the status of the laity in the Church arises in the most practical way. For as long as I can contribute advice and work, but am excluded from decision-making, I remain, no matter how many fine things are said about my status, a second-class member of this community: I am more an object which is utilized than a subject who is actively responsible. The person who can advise and collaborate, but not participate in decision-making in a manner befitting that person's status, *is* not really the Church, but only *belongs to* the Church. Yet this idea contradicts the very understanding of "laity" as we have once again seen it in the past decades, not least in Vatican II itself. It is not necessary here to go into the problematic of the somewhat unfortunate term "laity"; we not infrequently compensate for it by the use of such terms as "church" or "congregation," in contrast to the "shepherds" (presiding officers) or the "pastoral offices" (the supervisory offices).

Unfortunately the Decree on the Apostolate of the Laity of Vatican II, which carries on in a very longwinded and paternal fashion about various subjects which are quite obvious, remains on this point, which is so decisive in practical life, far behind what Yves Congar had already pioneered with concrete possibilities in the difficult preconciliar days by his courageous and epoch-making *"Jalons pour une théologie du laïcat."*[1] Did this happen solely because this Decree on the Apostolate of the Laity came about without the active participation of the laity itself in the decision-making, and thus is essentially a product of clerics? Well, even Yves Congar is not a layman, but a cleric. That the decree has here a blind spot should not so much be ascribed to the clergy *qua* clergy as to the clericalism of the clergy, a trait which can also be found among the laity.

The basis for joint decision in the Church was itself laid out thoroughly in the decree, in as much as in the first section of the first preparatory chapter it was said that the laity "share in the priestly, prophetic, and royal office of Christ" and that from thence they "have their own role to play in the mission of the whole people of God in the Church and in the world" (2). And at the same time the decree alludes to the pertinent section of the Constitution on the Church, which will be reproduced here in full, because it explains in a concise, beautiful, and constructive way the basis on which our later reflections are grounded:

Therefore, the chosen people of God is one: "one Lord, one faith, one baptism" (Eph. 4:5). As members, they share a common dignity from their rebirth in Christ. They have the same filial grace and the same vocation to perfection. They possess in common one salvation, one hope, and one undivided charity. Hence, there is in Christ and in the Church no inequality on the basis of race or nationality, social condition or sex, because "there is neither Jew nor Greek; there is neither slave nor freeman; there is neither male nor female. For you are all "one" in Christ Jesus" (Gal. 3:28; cf. Col. 3:11).

If therefore everyone in the Church does not proceed by the same path, nevertheless all are called to sanctity and have received an equal privilege of faith through the justice of God (cf. 2 Pet. 1:1). And if by the will of Christ some are made teachers, dispensers of mysteries, and shepherds on behalf of others, yet all share a true equality with regard to the dignity and to the activity common to all the faithful for the building up of the Body of Christ.

---

[1] Yves Congar, *Jalons pour une théologie du laïcat* (Paris, 1953); *Lay People in the Church* (Westminster, Md., 1957).

For the distinction which the Lord made between sacred ministers and the rest of the people of God entails a unifying purpose, since pastors and the other faithful are bound to each other by a mutual need. Pastors of the Church, following the example of the Lord, should minister to one another and to the other faithful. The faithful in their turn should enthusiastically lend their cooperative assistance to their pastors and teachers. Thus in their diversity all bear witness to the admirable unity of the Body of Christ. This very diversity of graces, ministries, and works gathers the children of God into one, because "all these things are the work of one and the same Spirit" (1 Cor. 12:11).[2]

Now if all this is true — and it is — then the question arises spontaneously: If the community of all those in the Church goes so deep in spite of all differences of gifts and services that it can't go deeper, then why, considering the communality of the one Lord, of the one Spirit and the one Body, of one faith and one baptism, of one grace and vocation, of one hope and love and finally of one responsibility and task — why then, despite all the diversity of functions is there not also in the Church a communality of *decision*? On this one point the Constitution on the Church as well as the Decree on the Apostolate of the Laity remains timid. The medieval and post-Tridentine past still casts its long heavy shadows upon them. It was in fact seen as great progress that the laity, who since Trent, or actually only since Vatican I, had been excluded from the Councils, were again admitted at least in trifling numbers as auditors (the listening Church!). Vatican I was a council of the pope, Vatican II a council of the bishops (and the theologians); as such they were great councils. But only Vatican III, it remains to hope, will be a council of priests and laity. The bishops fought courageously for collegiality: but only on the level of the universal Church over against papal

---

[2]See the very helpful article by F. Klostermann, "Allgemeine Pastoraltheologie der Gemeinde," in *Handbuch der Pastoraltheologie* III (Freiburg-Basel-Vienna, 1968), p. 43: "For this reason there also exists that fundamental collegiality and conciliarity in the congregation, the community of Christ, of which we have already spoken. Therefore no one in the Church is only a presiding officer and no one is only a subordinate. Therefore behind and before every special calling in the community there is a common, basic Christian calling and a common, basic Christian status, in which everyone is reverend, excellent and eminent, in which everyone is spiritual (Rom. 8) and everyone 'ecclesiastical,' even if the current ecclesiastical law book still always speaks with predilection of clerics as 'ecclesiastici.' Therefore in the Church there must be brotherliness, conversation, joint responsibility of all for all, partnership and dialogue. Consequently even the highest hierarchs are never simply vis-à-vis the community, but at the same time are always fellow Christians, fellow students, fellow servants, as Augustine said, to whom still another service has been entrusted, as a different one has to another person, without, nevertheless, their losing all their fundamental equality."

absolutism (Papalism), and not on the level of the diocese over against its own similarly entrenched episcopal absolutism (Episcopalism). Here is the task of the future, which some bishops already perceive! The Constitution on the Church (especially 33–38) — and very much less clearly the Decree on the Apostolate of the Laity (especially 10, 20, 23–26), which was also decided upon by the hierarchy — speaks of course at great length and often still in an extremely paternalistic manner (with "fatherly love" the laity are addressed as the extensions and representatives of the clergy) of the much desired activity and collaboration of the laity, of involvement and encouragement, recognition and the fostering of the laity, of the usefulness of their advice and their experience. How laboriously and repeatedly the "concessions" to the laity had to be wrung almost word by word from the traditionalistic curial group for the decree on the laity as well as for the chapter on the laity in the Constitution on the Church is impressively shown by the excellent commentary by Ferdinand Klostermann.[3]

There is also in the documents repeated talk of possible agencies or lay councils (e.g., Constitution on the Church, 37; Decree on the Apostolate of the Laity, 26), which, however, according to the assertions of the documents seem to have no more than an advisory function. The following passage from the Constitution on the Church is typical of the great openness and at the same time the time-bound narrowness of Vatican II:

> Let sacred pastors recognize and promote the dignity as well as the responsibility of the layman in the Church. Let them willingly make use of his prudent advice. Let them confidently assign duties to him in the service of the Church, allowing him freedom and room for action. Further, let them encourage the layman so that he may undertake tasks on his own initiative. Attentively in Christ, let them consider with fatherly love the projects, suggestions, and desires proposed by the laity. Furthermore, let pastors respectfully acknowledge that just freedom which belongs to everyone in this earthly city.
>
> A great many benefits are to be hoped for from this familiar dialogue between the laity and their pastors: in the laity, a strengthened sense of personal responsibility, a renewed enthusiasm, a more ready application of their talents to the projects of their pastors. The latter, for their part, aided by the experience of the laity,

---

[3]F. Klostermann, in *Lexikon für Theologie und Kirche: Das Zweite Vatikanische Konzil: Konstitutionen, Dekrete und Erklärungen* (Freiburg-Basel-Vienna, 1966/67), I, 260–283; II, 585–701.

can more clearly and more suitably come to the decisions regarding spiritual and temporal matters. In this way, the whole Church, strengthened by each one of its members, can more effectively fulfill its mission for the life of the world (37).

The passage says much which was never found before in this form in official documents, and to that extent there has been a breakthrough to a new communality and community in the Church. But the passage is also steadfastly silent on the question which must not be avoided or overlooked: if the laity are to be included as advisors and collaborators, then why not also as decision-makers?

Fundamental Principles

But are there perhaps serious theological objections, and not merely a centuries-long tradition of clericalism in the Catholic Church, which do indeed favor the participation of the laity in advising and working, but not in decision-making in the Church? Is this not perhaps a misunderstanding of the real essence of the Church, which is grounded not on a free accord of a believing individual, but on the call by God in Christ? Has not an essential differentness — a differentness which does not admit a transference of the modern democratic model to the Church — been overlooked? Has not the hierarchical character of the Church, which is built upon the Apostles and the apostolic succession of the office-bearers and thus excludes any democratization, been forgotten? These and similar serious considerations should be answered, and of course not simply from the conciliar decrees, which in their treatment of this question have remained superficial, but from the original Christian message, as it expressed itself and operated in the Church or the churches of the original New Testament age. What was originally correct cannot later on be rejected as false in principle by those who call themselves followers.

1. If we may, to begin with, argue from a more sociological point of view: some of those who today reject joint-decision-making with the laity in the Church earlier rejected on the same basis any serious participation of the laity through collaboration and advising in the Church. And some of those who protest today against a democratization of the Church and against any transference of secular sociological models to the Church not too long ago accepted without reflection the secular sociological model of the monarchy for the Church, and even in practice did nothing against the monarchization of the Church. They found no contradiction to the brotherhood of the New

Testament[4] in conducting themselves in practice as monarchs, for the most part bound in no way by a constitution, but for all practical purposes absolute monarchs: petty and sometimes even very great and mighty kings and lords in their parishes ("monsignor," i.e., "My Lord"), dioceses ("Your Grace," "Excellency," and "Eminence"), and in the universal Church ("Summus Pontifex" and "King of Kings and Lord of Lords"). This is not to say anything against the past, but it is past! In some countries Catholics even in this century opposed in every way possible the introduction of democratic forms into secular society in the name of this "divinely established" monarchical hierarchy, and Leo XIII was actually disgracefully insulted by ultra-Catholics when he finally abandoned the scruples of the hierarchical Church toward the democratic form of government. In a nutshell: The man who has nothing against the monarchization of the Church can really not have any decisive theological objection to the democratization of the Church. Basically it is better even in the Church to speak of a democracy (the entire holy people of God) than of the "hierocracy" (a holy caste). For while in the New Testament all worldly honorary titles are strictly shunned in connection with bearers of office, they are in fact given to the entire believing people, which is designated "a chosen race, a royal priesthood, a consecrated nation" (1 Pet. 2:9), and made "a line of kings and priests, to serve our God and to rule the world" (Rev. 5:10).

But that already demonstrates that in decisive matters we are careful to argue not in sociological but in theological categories. Only in this way can we show that joint decision-making and regulation on the part of the laity is not only a timely concession to modern democratic developments, but is a move thoroughly rooted in the Church's own origins. This is not to deny that the modern democratic development has not ultimately helped the Church break out of her traditionalistic clerical encrustations and reflect on her original structure. Here a comparison with the democratic state can be helpful: as citizens not only belong to the State, but in a full sense *are* the State, so all Church members in a full sense are the Church; they are all not mere inhabitants but full citizens of the Church. Instead of this, the traditional concept of the Church with its two-class theory, especially as it has operated since the Constantinian era in the entire ecclesiastical area, and after the Gregorian reform in its ultra-clerical form, has relied mostly on other models. Among these models were the monarchist state (more frequently of an

---

[4]See the recent article by E. Golomb, "Kirchenstruktur Brüderlichkeit," *Wort und Wahrheit* 23 (1968), 291–305.

imperial-absolute style): ruler and ruled, commander and subordinates; or the family: adults and minors, fathers and children; or the school: teachers and pupils (listeners); or property: owners (masters) and non-owners (servants).[5]

But can it be that the essence of the Church seen from a theological perspective necessarily demands two classes or ranks, especially as the Code of Canon Law in Canon 107 orders that "by virtue of divine institution" the clerics are to be differentiated from the laity in the Church?[6] A further clarification is necessary.

2. Out of a correct — that is to say, biblical and historical — perspective of "apostolic successions" there arises the question of the joint role of the laity in the decision-making in the Church.[7] Here this can be indicated only briefly.[8] The special and unquestionable apostolic succession of the multiple pastoral service (the bishops with the pope, but in their way also the pastors with their co-workers) must not be isolated, but must be seen in its functionality:

[5]What N. Greinacher says in "Der Vollzug der Kirche im Bistum," in *Handbuch der Pastoraltheologie* III (Freiburg-Basel-Vienna, 1968), p. 106, concerning the diocese is valid also for the parish and the universal Church: "There often still stands in the way of the realization of brotherliness and collegiality in the diocese a *paternalism* that is profoundly unchristian. For God himself has made an end to paternity on earth — there may yet be a physical, vicarious kind — as his Son entered as our brother into humanity and its history. It is time therefore to make an end to a paternalism that is socially obsolete as well as essentially unchristian. Brotherliness and paternalism in the Church are mutually exclusive. The very difficult question arises of whether Christian brotherliness does not slide into the background in the Church to the same degree as the notion of the father in reference to the pope, bishops and priests pushes to the fore. W. Dirks is correct in saying, 'If the Evangelical Church is threatened more by excessive fraternal confusion, in the Catholic Church it is the Father-image, the fear of brotherhood, which threatens the Word of Christ in history.'

[6]See the very illuminating article by J. Neumann, "Das 'jus divinum' im Kirchenrecht," in *Orientierung* 31 (1967), 5–8.

[7]On apostolic succession see besides the usual works on the Church in the New Testament (by O. Linton and F. M. Braun, and the monographs by F. J. Leenhardt, N. A. Dahl, O. Michel, G. Johnston, W. Robinson, A. Oepke, G. Aulén, L. G. Champion, A. Nygren, P. Minear, K. H. Schelkle, R. Schnackenburg, L. Cervaux) the more specialized researches by Ph. H. Menoud, *L'Eglise et le ministère selon le NT* (Neuchâtel, 1949); G. W. H. Lampe, *Some Aspects of the NT Ministry* (London, 1949); H. von Campenhausen, *Kirchliches Amt und geisliche Vollmacht in den ersten drei Jahrhunderten* (Tübingen, 1953); H. Schlier, *Die Zeit der Kirche* (Freiburg i. Br., 1955), 129–147; G. Dix, *Le Ministère dans l'élise ancienne* (Neuchâtel-Paris, 1955); E. Schweizer, *Gemeinde und Gemeindeordnung im NT* (Zürich, 1959); E. Käsemann, *Exegetische Versuche und Besinnungen* I (Göttingen, 1960), 109–134; H. U. von Balthasar, *Sponsa Verbi* (Einsiedeln, 1960), 80–147; E. Schlink, *Der kommende Christus und die kirchlichen Traditionen* (Göttingen, 1961), 160–195; for literature from the fields of history and systematic theology on the subject of ecclesiastical office, see H. Küng, *Structures of the Church* (New York, 1964), chapter 6 (includes a response to the positions of Käsemann and Schlink), and the pertinent lexicon articles.

[8]For the basic foundation of all that follows see H. Küng, *The Church* (New York, 1968), chapter E.

a. The Church *as a whole* (*Credo Ecclesiam apostolicam!*), and thus each individual church member, also stands in succession to the apostles. In what sense? The Church, as well as all individuals, remains bound to the basic witness and service of the original witnesses without which there would be no Church. The Church is founded on the apostles (and the prophets). All the faithful thus are supposed to succeed the apostles in apostolic faith and confessing, life and service. This service takes the most diverse forms of proclamation, baptism, the community of prayer and the Supper, the building up of the congregation, and service to the world.

b. The special apostolic succession of the diverse *pastoral service*, important as it is, is not thereby an end in itself. The pastoral service continues the special task of the apostles, which differs from other important and likewise permanent services in the Church, such as that of the prophets or the teachers: namely, to establish and guide the Churches. From this service of guiding the Church, these office bearers (bishops, pastors, further co-workers) also have a special authority; only in service can their authority have any foundation at all. The shepherds in the Church are thus in no way a management class with a unilateral imperial power, toward which the single possible attitude is unilateral obedience. They are no *dominium*, but a *ministerium*. They form no power-structure but a special service-structure. "You know that among the pagans their so-called rulers lord it over them, and their great men make their authority felt. This is not to happen among you. No; anyone who wants to become great among you must be your servant, and anyone who wants to be first among you must be slave to all. For the Son of Man himself did not come to be served but to serve, and to give his life as a ransom for many" (Mark 10:42–45).

So the purpose of shepherds in the Church is special service to the apostolic Church which is made up of all the believers. For this reason the term "hierarchy" or "holy rule" (customary only since the time of Dionysius the Pseudo-Areopagite five hundred years after Christ) is misleading. To be relevant biblically, it is better to speak of "diakonia" or "church service."

For the nurturing and constant growth of the people of God, Christ the Lord instituted in His Church a variety of ministries, which work for the good of the whole body. For those ministers who are endowed with sacred power are servants of their brethren, so that all who are of the people of God, and therefore enjoy a true Christian dignity, can work toward a common goal freely and in an orderly way, and arrive at salvation. (Constitution on the Church, 18)

Thus if from a biblical perspective the shepherds are not the masters but the servants of the Church or the congregation (= the "laity"), why then should it in practice be possible to exclude the Church or the congregation (= the "laity") from joint decision-making? This can happen only if the shepherds are seen not as the servants of the Church but as its exclusive owners or fathers or teachers.

But the shepherds are *not* the *owners* of the Church, toward whom laity are only dependents who have nothing to say in the management. The Church is not a huge industry: all members of the Church *are* Church, the Church belongs to all of them, and the shepherds are also *not* the *fathers* of the Church, in contrast to whom the laity are only minors who still cannot have any responsibility of their own for the Church. The Church cannot be considered simply as a family (except as under God, the one Father): all grown-up members of the Church are adult members who have an established inalienable responsibility for the whole. And, finally, the shepherds are also *not* the *teachers* of the Church, in contrast to whom the laity are only learning pupils who have only to listen and to obey. The Church is not a school: all Church members have "learnt from God" (1 Thess. 4:9) and "do not need anyone to teach" them (1 John 2:27).

In brief: in the Church, despite all the variations of office, which we must return to, all are ultimately equal insofar as they all are believers and, as such, adult brothers and sisters under the one Father and the one Lord Jesus. Teaching and advising, like listening and obeying, are, because all members are filled by the Spirit, *reciprocal*. To this extent the Church, despite all differences of services, is no two-class society of possessor and nonpossessor, empowered and powerless, adults and minors, knowledgeable and ignorant, but a community of love filled and authorized by the Spirit in which only greater service bestows greater authority.

3. If then within this community of basic equality the variety of services and the special fullness of power of the pastoral office are nevertheless to be taken seriously, the question of the relation of the Church (the local church or parish, the diocesan church, the universal Church) to the relevant pastoral office (pastor and his co-workers, bishop, pope) must be defined anew: does the universal fullness of power of the Church confirm the particular fullness of power of the pastoral office or is it the other way around — does the particular fullness of power of the pastoral

office confirm the universal fullness of power of the Church? This must be examined carefully.

a. The joint decision-making of the laity in the Church can obviously *not be founded* on the fact that the fullness of power of the shepherds is derived simply from the fullness of power of the Church or congregation, from the fullness of power of the universal priesthood. Then the special pastoral office would simply be leveled within the Church and within the universal priesthood: an unbiblical democratization!

b. But on the other hand the participation of the laity in the decision-making of the Church can also *not* be *excluded* on the basis that the fullness of power of the Church or congregation is simply derived from the fullness of power of the shepherd, as though the shepherds alone stood in succession to the apostles and were not the servants of the Church but its masters or mediators. Thus the pastoral service would be isolated from the Church or congregation, from the universal priesthood, and its apostolic succession would be absolutized: an unbiblical hierarchicalization or clericalization of the Church!

c. If, however, as we say, the Church and her shepherds all stand together under the one Father and Lord, who makes them all brothers, if they all stand under the one message of Christ and all are called into the same discipleship and the same obedience to God and his Word; if ultimately they are all the hearing Church and precisely as hearers are all filled with the Spirit, then it follows that the fullness of power of the Church or congregation is not derived from the fullness of power of the shepherds, and the fullness of power of the shepherds is not derived from the fullness of power of the Church or congregation, but the fullness of power of *both* is directly derived from the fullness of power of the Lord of the Church in his Spirit. This common origin of their fullness of power establishes the universal authorization of the congregation as well as the special fullness of power of the service of the shepherds. It is the support of the authority of the shepherds as well as of the participation of the "laity" in decision-making.

4. The joint decision-making of the "laity" in the Church will, then, be seen correctly only if Church or congregation and the shepherds are seen as intimately related as well as different. It is this perspective which eliminates all absolutistic decision-making by either the shepherd *or* the congregation alone, which excludes both ecclesiastical oligarchy (monarchy) *and* ochlocracy. If, as we have emphasized, the universal priesthood, if the various charismatic gifts and offices, and if especially the charismata of the prophets and teachers are taken seriously in the Church, then the *special office of the shepherds* (presiding officers) in the Church must and will also be taken very seriously: it is the special voca-

tion of individual believing persons (in principle — for there is no biblical or dogmatic objection to it — both men and women) to the permanent and regular (not only occasional), public (not only private) service to the congregation as such (and not only to individual members) through the laying on of hands or ordination (and not only through the equally possible charism of the Spirit breaking through as He wills).

From this *special* service the shepherds have also *special* authority which can never be simply eliminated or passed over in the Church or congregation. From this special *service*, however, they have their authority only within, for, and in collaboration with the Church or congregation. So the *shepherds from the very outset are oriented to the joint collaboration, decision-making, and regulating of the congregation.* This orientation does not mean a constraint and restriction, but a protection against all stifling isolation, a help in all their need, a liberation into true togetherness. The shepherds must see their special fullness of power embedded and protected in the universal authorization of the Church and of each individual church member. Solitary responsibility stifles, common responsibility sustains.

The Word, baptism, the Eucharist, forgiveness, the office of love are given to the entire Church. But a few must discharge the service of the Word, the sacrament, and the Church permanently, regularly, and publicly in the Church, strengthened and legitimized for this through prayer and the power of ordination, which itself should occur in cooperation with the entire Church. Concretely: *all* Christians are empowered to preach the Word and to witness to the faith in the Church and in the world; but only to the shepherds of the congregation who are called, or to those delegated by them, is the special fullness of power to preach in the congregational assembly given. *All* Christians are empowered to exhort people to forgive their brothers and sisters in a crisis of conscience; but only to those called as shepherds is given the special fullness of power of the words of reconciliation and absolution, which is exercised in the congregational assembly upon the congregation and thus upon the individuals. For the co-execution of baptism and the Eucharist *all* Christians are authorized; but only to those called as shepherds is given the special fullness of power to perform baptisms in public in the congregation and to conduct responsibly the congregational Eucharist.

5. Thus of their innermost essence the Church or congregation and the shepherds are oriented toward one another in decision-making. On the basis of their special mission with which they step before the congregation, the ordained shepherds have a pre-established authority in the Church or the congregation. On the basis of their ordination the shepherds need not demonstrate their vocation, like every other charis-

matic, by the exhibition of their charism (in proof of the Spirit and the power). Rather they are appointed from the very beginning: legitimized as the ones who are fully authorized for this office in a special way for the public activity of the congregation in the Spirit. But this must not be misunderstood, as though the shepherds ultimately were raised over the congregation to become the lords of the congregation, where they no longer remained dependent on the congregation. Every time shepherds play up their own persons, every time they think and act autocratically, conduct themselves tyrannically and autonomously, they betray the mission which they have received. They fail to understand that their special mission is a charism, a call from the Spirit to gain which they can do nothing, which has been given them without their earning it. They are straying from the gospel which they have been called to serve and which demands of them that they serve others. All this would be an error and a fault in them, and the congregation and each Christian would be justified and called upon by the Spirit to show their opposition through open witness, provided they acted in truth and love. If however the special mission of the shepherd is received in faith, embraced each day with new fidelity, and exercised in love, then it must also give to those sent the certainty that they have been truly sent with authority, the confidence that they can measure up to the call despite all personal weakness, the courage to attack the task anew again and again and to proclaim the Word of God whether it is opportune or inopportune, the inner calm, despite all temptations, to endure to the end all crises and all assaults: "That is why I am reminding you now to fan into a flame the gift (charisma) that God gave you when I laid my hands on you. God's gift was not a spirit of timidity, but the Spirit of power, and love, and self-control. So you are never to be ashamed of witnessing to the Lord . . ." (2 Tim. 1:6–8).

So the shepherds and the congregation have their mutual obligations: the shepherds have the duty and the task to proclaim the Christian message to the congregation again and again, even when it is uncomfortable for the congregation. The congregation, on the other hand, has the duty and the task of retesting again and again whether the shepherds are remaining true to their commission, whether they are acting according to the gospel. For there are not only false prophets, but also faithless shepherds. And if the Pauline statement "Never try to suppress the Spirit or treat the gift of prophecy with contempt" (1 Thess. 5:19f.) holds true especially for the presiding officers, then what follows certainly holds true not only for some presiding officers, but for the entire congregation and each individual — "Think before you do anything — hold on to what is good and avoid every form of evil" (1 Thess. 5:21f.).

Thus everyone is helped by this mutual respectful examination, this reciprocal criticism without disputation, this universal *correctio fraterna* in modesty. And all this is a presupposition for common action, for which all that we have said is basically true: no individual decisions, neither of the Church or congregation nor of the shepherd! No going-it-alone, either of the "laity" without the shepherd or of the shepherd without the "laity." No sole control, neither dictatorship of the one nor dictatorship of the many! Instead of seclusion and isolation, openness and solidarity. Instead of paternalism, brotherliness. Instead of autocracy and deposition, service and love. Instead of servitude, freedom; instead of egotistic power, existence for others.[9]

6. If common responsibility, if joint-decision-making of the congregation with the shepherd is seen in this way, then one need have no anxiety for the order of the congregation, even if it is threatened again and again from all sides. Then a first principle will be true for the shepherd as well as for the members of the congregation: to each his own! Then the shepherd will not assume a superiority over the congregation nor the congregation over the shepherd. Then neither shepherd nor laity will wish to commandeer and subordinate everything for themselves, but they will each give and relinquish what belongs to the other. And then a second principle is valid: *with one another for one another!* Then neither the shepherd nor laity will use their fullness of power as a weapon against the other in order to grasp a position for themselves and seize the power in the Church, but they will use this fullness of power in the only way it makes sense, to serve one another and the whole. And finally there is one supreme criterion: *obedience to the Lord!* Then neither the shepherd nor the laity will play the role of Lord of the Church, but find true freedom, imperturbable peace, and a permanent joy even amid difficulties and affliction in subordination to the one Lord and his Word in love.

---

[9]See Greinacher, p. 106f.: "If we are in earnest when we speak of Christian brotherliness and the equality of the members of the diocese, we must move toward a far-reaching *democratization of the structures of the Church*. Such a democratization corresponds on the one hand to an original and genuine stream of Christian tradition in the Church and on the other hand also to the mentality and the structures of contemporary secular society, which, as we have shown, cannot conceal its own Christian origins. One thing must be clear: one cannot speak of the co-responsibility of the laity if participation in *decision-making* is not granted. The summons of the laity to co-responsibility and care for the diocese has meaning really only if this laity is also guaranteed a genuine role in diocesan decision-making. If this is not the case, then one not unjustly runs the danger that this summons to joint care will be regarded as a farce. If the complaint is heard so often that the laity show so slight an interest in the call to participation in the apostolate, then it should be asked whether the necessary place has also been made for their role in decision-making. Only under this condition of genuine participation in decision-making will it be possible in the long run to integrate the laity into the Church in any authentic way."

In this way a correct perspective on *obedience* in the Church is also possible. For Paul, the service that actually occurs is the reason why subordination to those who make great exertions is obligatory. Those who always volunteer for a special service — not only that of the shepherd, but also of the prophet or teacher or helper etc. — and prove themselves in it, have the call of God, they have received the gift of grace of the Spirit. It is not simply a certain station, not a special tradition, not great age, not a long membership in the congregation, not even finally a conferring of the Spirit, but service itself perfected in the Spirit which creates authority in the congregation. Thus the obedience of everyone to God, Christ, the Spirit is demanded: here *unconditional* obedience is valid. But toward other people, whose will after all is certainly not always in accord with the will of God, there is even in the Church only a *conditional* and never a unilateral obedience. Free reciprocal subordination, free service of all for all, free obedience toward the always-other gifts of grace of the other, is the consequence of obedience of all to God, Church, the Spirit. The one Lord acts in one Spirit not only through the shepherds but through all the various gifts of grace (1 Cor. 12:4–6). And the whole life of the Church will thus be a united living ensemble of shepherds and congregation, including all the various spiritual gifts and offices, amid which order and peace should rule — and yet the Spirit must never be muffled.

Embodiment

The embodiment of an ecclesiastical order which is justified by the original Christian message and Church must be different for different times and different places. In every case a transposition is necessary. Thus it is far from our intention to deliver a hard unhistorical judgment on times in which this ecclesiastical order was realized only very imperfectly.[10] And likewise it is not our intention to give a simple prescription for a universal remedy the better to realize such a truly Christian order in all the varied areas of the Church. Nevertheless attention ought to be called to a few points of a general nature.

Precisely what are the concrete possibilities for the participation of the laity in the decision-making of the Church? Yves Congar has called attention to the most important in the above-mentioned book.[11]

---

[10]Peter Stockmeier, "Gemeinde und Bischofsamt in der alten Kirche," *Theologische Quartalschrift* (Tübingen) 149, no. 2 (1969), 133–146, shows of course that the constitution of the ancient Church was very much closer, and not only just in time, to the original Christian message and Church than was the constitution of the post-Tridentine Church.

[11]Congar, *Jalons pour une théologie du laïcat*, 329–333.

1. the role of the laity in elections, and the occupying of ecclesiastical offices;

2. the role of the laity in councils;

3. the role of the princes in the Church;

4. the role of the congregation in the ordering of their own life through the law of use and custom;

5. the participation of the laity in the administration of church property and in ecclesiastical jurisdiction.

The role of the laity in the Council we have treated in detail on another occasion.[12] In view of the contemporary postconciliar situation, continuing Congar's thought and at the same time following certain items in the Council documents themselves, we can mention two ways in which the participation of the laity in decision-making can be concretized: first in the collegial Church leadership on the various levels and then also in the free election of presiding officers through a representation of the pertinent churches.[13]

1. *The collegial Church leadership on the various levels.*

The "collegiality" emphasized by the Council, that is the brotherly-communal character of Church leadership, must not arbitrarily remain limited to the uppermost level of the universal Church (pope, bishops). It must also be realized on the level of the national church, the diocesan church, and above all the local church (and correspondingly also in the religious orders with their lay brothers). That means very clearly a dissolution of that authoritarian one-man rule — whether on the level of the parish, bishopric, nation, or the universal Church — which, as we have seen, is consonant neither with the original New Testament organization nor with contemporary democratic thought.

According to what we have already said about the shepherds, it is quite clear that the decisive authority of the pastor, the bishop, and the pope should remain explicitly preserved; only in this way can the mutual paralysis of the various powers normally be avoided. Nevertheless at the same time not only collaboration and counselling but also participation in decision-making by representative councils of the churches in question should be guaranteed. In order that these councils be truly representative it is necessary that the greater part of the members be elected in free and secret elections; a minority can be members *ex officio* because

---

[12]Küng, *Structures of the Church*, chapter 5.

[13]The notions raised here are developed in a more general context in *Truthfulness the Future of the Church* (New York, 1968), chapter B, IX.

of certain important service functions or through their nomination by responsible shepherds (pastor, bishop, bishops' conference, or pope).

The constitutional foundations for these pressing and incisive reforms are laid down, at least for the diocese, by the Council itself: it was resolved by Vatican II that in every diocese a diocesan pastoral council should be established, to be composed of priests, religious, and laity. This pastoral council is already a reality in some dioceses, wherein the priests' council, also decreed by the Council, is partly integrated into this pastoral council, and the laity often have a two-thirds majority. In the concrete statutes of the diocesan council, care must be taken to assure that a true participation in decision-making is guaranteed, in which a kind of veto power (or a necessity of agreement) can be vested in the authorized shepherd. An appearance of collegiality, which admits no true participation of the council in decision-making, can do more harm than good; it is nothing but the collegial cloak for the old princely absolutism. Thus — a warning example to other levels — it was depressing to see how already at the first episcopal synod in Rome after the Council, true collegiality was completely overruled by the old papal absolutism: the things to be settled were unilaterally established and narrowed by the curial side, the most pressing problems of the universal Church (like birth control and celibacy) could not be discussed, no experts were admitted, much was discussed and resolved, but nothing was decided; the bishops travelled home without knowing which of these agreements the pope and the curial apparatus would bring to realization; practically speaking, the bishops' synod had no serious immediate effects.

As in the diocese, collegial leadership of the Church must also be realized on the other levels:

a. For the universal Church this would mean setting up a lay council parallel to the bishops' council which is already constituted, though still not permanent, still not assembling regularly, and still with no authority. This could come about as a result of the international lay congress, which in the postconciliar period showed more vitality, courage, and resolution than the synod of bishops. This lay council, together with the bishops' council under the decisive leadership of the pope (the veto power), could not only give advice but also decide on the important concerns of the universal Church.

b. For each nation there should be set up, again paralleling the diocesan pastoral council, a national pastoral council, consisting of bishops, priests, and laity, for counselling and communal decision-making in all important concerns of the national Church.

c. For every parish there should be set up, where this has not already happened, a parish council of men and women, paralleling the diocesan pastoral council, for the purposes of counselling and participation in decision-making with the pastor (who would have veto power) in all important parish concerns.

For the concrete statute the following should be observed:

a. In all the decision-making councils we have described, from the parish council to the lay senate and the bishops' council of the entire Church, it should be self-explanatory that a sufficient number of qualified *women* are also to be admitted as members. Such representation is a part of the full participation of women in the life of the Church on the basis of equality. On the various levels care must be taken eventually for the education and inclusion of women in active co-responsibility.

b. On every level theological and other *professional people* are to be drawn in, corresponding to the scholarly areas under discussion.

c. For practical functioning the American principle of "checks and balances," which precludes a monopolization of power in certain hands, is helpful. In the United States the president as well as Congress has a strong position. And so ultimately the president can do nothing without Congress, and Congress can do nothing without the president. The executive branch (the president) can employ a strong initiative and in emergency even a strong brake. But it is bound by the resolutions of the legislative branch (Congress), against which the president can — but in practice seldom does — apply a veto. Moreover, both the president and Congress are controlled by the judiciary branch (the courts). So the president and Congress mutually hinder and help one another. Autocracy and the dictatorship of an individual are avoided, as are ochlocracy and the fragmentation of the many, all of which benefits both the freedom of the individual and the well-being of the whole.[14]

2. *Free election of presiding officers by a representation of the pertinent churches.*

This should hold true for pastors, bishops, and pope. Such an election can be arranged with the cooperation of the representative councils discussed above, to which, circumstances permitting, other members can be co-opted for the electoral college: for the election of the pope in the universal Church the bishops' council and lay council would be duly qualified, for the election of the bishop in the diocese the diocesan pastoral council, for the election of the pastor in the local Church the parish council (or as in some Swiss cantons, the assembled congregation).

In the election of the pastor and bishops a control function would belong to the superior pastoral offices: the election of pastors would have

---

[14]Further possibilities of cooperation between presiding officers and congregation are discussed by A. Müller and R. Völkel, "Die Funktion der Laien in der Pfarrgemeinde," in *Handbuch für Pastoraltheologie* III (Freiburg-Basel-Vienna, 1968), pp. 233–253.

to be approved by the bishops, the election of bishops by the episcopal conference in its majority or by the pope. In this way the old axioms of canon law would once again hold good and could be applied by analogy to all ecclesiastical offices: "No bishop should be installed against the will of the people" (Pope Celestine I) and "He who presides over all should be elected by all" (Pope Leo the Great).

As to concrete regulations, several points would be important:

a. Election not only of the superiors of religious orders, or, as in certain church areas, the pastor, but also of the bishops and all office-holders for a substantial but stipulated time (e.g., six or eight years with the possibility of re-election) is both a justified and urgent desideratum in today's situation.

b. Directives for obligatory (e.g., at seventy years) or optional (e.g., at sixty-five years) resignation from ecclesiastical offices are necessary. On the other side, demands of a congregation for the retirement of a shepherd should never be legally binding without the agreement of the superior office-holder (bishop for the pastor, pope or episcopal conference for the bishop); in this way illegitimate attempts at pressure can be averted from the pertinent administrator.

c. A special committee should advise the bishop in all personnel concerns; such a group can consider each case carefully — the special peculiarities and requisites of the position concerned as well as the wishes of the congregation and of the person in question. Special attention must be given to the pastor-assistant relationship, which is full of vexation.

Only one example, though one which has central significance, shall be investigated here more closely: election of bishops.[15] The election of the bishop of Rome, the pope, will not be treated specially here; nevertheless it must be clear even without a long explanation how pressing is the transferral of the election from the College of Cardinals, which is in no way representative and in any case is anachronistic, to the episcopal and lay councils: today more than ever the pope needs the broadest consensus in the Church!

The election of the bishop by a representative council of the pertinent Church satisfies the following:

---

[15]On the election of bishops see besides the manuals on the history of canon law (especially E. Feine, W. Plöchl), the short summary by K. Mörsdorf in the article "Bischof III. Kirchenrechtlich," in *Lexikon für Theologie und Kirche* II (Freiburg i. Br., 1958), 497–505; Günter Biemer, "Die Bischofswahl als neues Desiderat kirchlicher Praxis," *Theologische Quartalschrift*, 149, no. 2 (1969), 171–184; Johannes Neumann, "Wahl und Amtszeitbegrenzung nach kanonischem Recht," ibid., 117–132; Stockmeier, "Gemeinde und Bischofsamt in der alten Kirche."

1. the theological as well as practical high esteem for the particular and local Church, for the diocese and the congregation (see esp. the Constitution on the Church, 26, and the Decree on the Bishops' Pastoral Office in the Church, e.g., 27);

2. the demand for decentralization, which stipulates a dismantling of the power of the Roman curia in favor of the churches in the individual nations (establishment of national bishops conferences, etc.; see Decree on the Bishops' Pastoral Office in the Church, e.g., 36–38);

3. the demand for a curial reform (which, unfortunately, has still not been radically accomplished), which will provide not a broadening of the area of curial competence over against the episcopates of individual countries, but on the contrary the insertion of representatives of the most varied countries into the ecclesiastical central administration (see Decree on the Bishops' Pastoral Office in the Church, 9–10);

4. the strict definition (which here would mean limitation) of the authority of the nuncio, as desired by the Council: "The Fathers also eagerly desire that, in view of the pastoral role proper to bishops, the office of legates of the Roman Pontiff be more precisely determined" (Decree on the Bishops' Pastoral Office in the Church, 9; cf. 10).

For a historical understanding of these conclusions of Vatican II it must be remembered that these conclusions doubtless stand in a clear front-line against Roman centralism, authoritarianism, and absolutism, as it has prevailed in the West since the Gregorian reform and the High Middle Ages and reached its unsurpassable high point in the period after Vatican I with the new codification of the Code of Canon Law. But on the basis of what has been stated here from the New Testament, it must be clear that these conclusions are not concerned with attempted "innovations," but with a return to tradition,[16] the truly good old tradition. The election of bishops is itself an excellent model for this, as it was earlier. In the election of bishops it was from the beginning kept in mind that not only a clerical hierarchy of functionaries but rather the entire community of believers, the entire people of God, is the Church.

The spirit of the resolutions of Vatican II means a reinclusion of

---

[16]See esp. Stockmeier, "Gemeinde und Bischofsamt in der alten Kirche."

clergy and laity in the election of bishops after the model of the ancient Church.[17]

In conclusion let us say only this: Obviously there is no perfect system of organization; in concrete life each has its specific defects and dangers. But a system better than that canonized by the present Code of Canon Law is not difficult to think of! [18] The one suggested here in some of its basic features corresponds better both to the original organization of the apostolic Church and to our contemporary democratic times.

[17]Greinacher, p. 107: "If it is correct that every believing Christian is a brother or sister of Jesus and that the Spirit of Christ operates in each, that the Spirit blows where it will, and that there is also charisma outside office, then the idea cannot be excluded that these Christians should also exert an influence on the fulfillment of the Church in the diocese and on the *filling of posts of service*. In the election of the apostle Matthias (Acts 15:22f.) as well as in the election of deacons (Acts 6:1–6), the collaboration of the entire community was considered self-explanatory (see also Acts 15:22f.). It is well-known that the leaders of the congregations in the first centuries up to the time of Ambrose and Augustine were determined with the collaboration of the congregation. Until recently the Church tolerated a situation in which the nobility exerted an influence on the filling of certain parish positions. Even up to the year 1903 the Church countenanced the fact that in practice the Kaiser influenced the papal elections. Up until our own time — and not only in Eastern countries — the governments in some countries exerted a massive influence on the episcopal elections. Would it not be more appropriate to give some influence in the filling of offices to everyone who is immediately concerned and who is co-responsible for the bishopric — namely, the members of the local church? Is it not time to give the old democratic tendencies in the Church another chance and endow them with a new meaning and a new expression which would be suitable for our time, which is characterized by the process of 'fundamental democratization'?"

[18]See esp. Biemer, "Die Bischofswahl als neues Desiderat kirchlicher Praxis," and Neumann, "Wahl und Amtszeitbegrenzung nach kanonischem Recht."

9

Free Election of Bishops:
A Concrete Model

As It Now Is

The Swiss diocese of Basel differs from most other dioceses in the world in that the bishop is elected by the diocesan clergy of the cathedral chapter alone, without any interference from official agencies in Rome. It is only afterward that Rome confirms the vote. The governing bodies of the local cantons therefore enjoy a limited power of veto, but this has not been exercised for a long time.

The legal basis for this election of the bishop in the diocese of Basel is the series of treaties between the governing bodies of the relevant cantons and the Holy See.[1] There is no doubt about the legal position of the cathedral chapter and the diocesan canons. The State treaty in question provides as follows: "The canons of the cathedral who constitute the episcopal senate have the right to elect the bishop from among the clergy of the diocese. The person elected bishop will be confirmed in office by the Holy Father as soon as the canonical formalities have been completed according to the forms of the Church customary in Switzerland" (compare art. 5). The Apostolic Bull of Leo XII of May 7, 1828, confirms this and adds that when the papal confirmation cannot for any reason follow, it is again not the pope but the cathedral chapter which must proceed to a new election.

It follows that the right of election belongs unequivocally to the cathedral senate of the diocese, which carries out the election without

---

[1]The treaties of March 26, 1828, contracted between the cantonal governments of Lucerne, Bern, Solothurn, and Zug and the Holy See, represented by the apostolic Internuncio Gizzi (to which should be added the treaty with Aargau in 1828, with Thurgau in 1929, and later with Basel).

consulting or informing Rome in any way. And the phrase "according to the forms of the Church customary in Switzerland" refers to that cooperation with the cantons of the diocese which was explicitly recognized in papal briefs: "The Church flourishes when government and priesthood agree together." What this means, according to the same brief of Leo XII dated September 15, 1828, is that no candidates should be elected who are *"gubernio minus grati,"* i.e., who are not acceptable to the cantonal governments.[2]

These ancient rights of the cathedral chapter and the cantons of the diocese alike which have been acknowledged by Rome in this way and which do not envisage Rome being involved in the information process to the slightest degree have, naturally, been respected in every episcopal election to date. They are comprehensively laid down in the *Statuta Capituli Ecclesiae Cathedralis Basilensis* which have been explicitly confirmed with only minor modifications in the recent codification of church law. These statutes[3] specify the method of election in a manner that acknowledges the traditional rights both of the diocesan cantons and of the cathedral chapter in a most emphatic way.

The election of the bishop must take place within three months.[4] The vicar of the cathedral chapter negotiates the choice of the date of the election with the governing bodies of the cantons.[5] Consultation with the governing bodies must be completed before the solemn vote.[6] In this way the chapter has to give precedence to the candidates who are not *"minus grati"*[7] Rome plays no part in this consultation. Where the election has to be repeated or where the pope does not approve, the chapter restarts the whole process.[8] The procedure of the election has to be strictly observed down to the last detail.[9] When the election has been completed, the provost of the cathedral or his deputy declares: "In my own name and in that of the cathedral senate of Basel I announce and proclaim that the Right Reverend N. N. has been elected to be bishop and pastor of the Church in Basel in the name of the Father, and of the Son, and of the Holy Spirit. Amen."[10] By way of conclusion the election has to be promulgated in the cathedral so that the *Te Deum* can

---

[2]See also the brief of December 16, 1831.
[3]See heading II, B on the election of the bishop.
[4]Art. 74.
[5]Arts. 75, 76.
[6]Art. 78.
[7]This can be established in various ways: See Art. 79 and the references therein cited to the relevant papal briefs.
[8]Art. 81, with its reference to the relevant brief of May 7, 1828.
[9]Arts. 82–89.
[10]Art. 90.

be solemnly sung and the election be closed with this festive song of thanks.[11] Should the person elected not be there, he should be informed of the election straightaway and asked whether he accepts.[12] He must signify this within eight days or else refuse.[13] The official authentication of the election, duly signed by all the elective members of the cathedral chapter, together with the necessary attestation of the qualification of the person elected, must then be sent to the pope in the usual way.[14] Once the Holy See has signified its approval, the solemn consecration of the bishop can follow.[15]

It is a matter for regret that on the occasion of the election of the last bishop (in 1967) the chapter yielded to the massive pressure from the Roman curia and the nunciature. Instead of announcing the result of the election in the way the concordat and custom required, the chapter bound itself under oath to silence, at first kept the name of the person elected secret, informed the curia instead of the clergy and the people, and secured its *nihil obstat* before it informed the person elected publicly. It was as if it were asking too much to expect the Holy See to ratify a perfectly legal election (and not a *fait accompli*). The incidental irony of the thing was that because of Rome's indiscretions the clergy and people had to get the name of the person elected, not from the cathedral chapter, as envisaged by the concordat, but from the press. We can only hope that for the next election there will be a strict adherence to the letter and the spirit of the concordat and to traditional procedure and that there is no yielding to pressure. For apart from the anachronistic (but nowadays harmless) possibility of interference by the State, the Basel regime stands out for having behind it not only Vatican II but an old Catholic tradition: The election of the bishop through a representative organ of the diocese.

We should note that both in its actual law and in its spirit this procedure anticipated much of what Vatican II set great store by (without, of course, drawing out the practical consequences for the election of bishops): (*a*) the theological and practical importance of the local and particular churches, the diocese, and the community;[16] (*b*) the furtherance of decentralization, which requires a divesting of power over the churches in individual countries on the part of the Roman curia;[17] (*c*) the furtherance of the reform of the curia, which is a matter not of widen-

---

[11] Art. 91.

[12] Art. 92.

[13] Art. 93.

[14] Art. 94.

[15] Art. 95.

[16] See in particular the Constitution on the Church, *Lumen Gentium*, 26, and the Decree on the Bishops' Pastoral Office in the Church, *Christus Dominus*, 27.

[17] The setting up of Episcopal Conferences, etc.; see *Christus Dominus*, 36–38.

ing the competence of the curia over the diocese of individual countries but, on the contrary, of the inclusion of representatives of the different countries in the central administration of the Church;[18] (*d*) the stricter delimitation or limitation of the powers of the nuncios as desired by the Council: "The Fathers also eagerly desire that, in view of the pastoral role proper to bishops, the office of legates of the Roman Pontiff be more precisely determined."[19]

As It Was

In order to understand these conclusions of Vatican II in historical perspective we should recall that they represent a bridgehead against Roman centralism, authoritarianism and absolutism as these have held sway in the West since the Gregorian reform and the High Middle Ages, and reached its highest point in the period after Vatican I with the new codification of canon law. At the same time these resolutions represent not daring "innovations" but a return to tradition, the good, old tradition. The election of bishops is precisely an outstanding example of how things used to be. From the very beginning the election of a bishop expressed the awareness that the Church is not a clerical hierarchy of office but the whole community of believers, the whole people of God. In primitive Christianity the bishop was elected by clergy and people. The greatest bishops in all times like Ambrose of Milan and Augustine of Hippo were decisively elected by the people. "*Nos eligimus eum*" — "We elect him" — ran the formula of the people's acclamation in the Latin countries. Nor was it the bishop of Rome but neighboring bishops who cooperated to give their sanction. The right to confirm and consecrate was given later, according to the definitions of the first ecumenical Council of Nicaea, not to the see of Rome but to the metropolitan of the relevant church province. We cannot here go into the way in which local princes later came to have a share in filling the bishop's see and the way in which the biblically grounded right of the ecclesial people came to be more and more restricted. The reform movement of the Middle Ages nevertheless demanded the free election of bishops and clergy and people (this was what Leo IX demanded at the Synod of Rome in 1049). The freedom of election of bishops was thoroughly secured at least in relation to the princes in the investiture struggle. At the same time, the ever-increasing power of the cathedral chapter meant that the lower clergy and the laity were correspondingly excluded. Whereas in the begin-

---

[18]See *Christus Dominus*, 9–10.
[19]*Christus Dominus*, 9; see also 10.

ning the cathedral chapter had only to agree to an election, it came more and more to determine it. The cathedral chapter's right of election was quite general by the end of the twelfth century and was laid down for the whole Church by the mightiest pope of the Middle Ages, Innocent III.

During the first few centuries the influence of the bishop of Rome on the election of bishops did not extend substantially further than the rights he enjoyed as metropolitan and patriarch, and it was only in the ninth century that he became involved regularly where there were complications (removal, replacement, conflicts about the election). But through the development favored by the papacy which we have sketched above, the right of confirmation and ordination fell more and more into the hands of the Roman see. From the High Middle Ages onward the right of ratification was often used to exert pressure on the electoral process. The end result was the system of reservations, according to which the popes kept the filling of the bishops' sees to themselves: first of all in isolated cases, then in certain specific sees and finally, from the fourteenth century onward (under the Avignon Pope Urban V, 1363) quite generally.

In this way the electoral right of the cathedral chapter was whittled away and in due course abolished by law. It was only after the Western schism and in the conflict over the Council of Basel that the cathedral chapter was again recognized through the Concordat of Vienna in 1448 to have at least a limited right to elect the bishop. This did not stop the development of a manifold right of nomination on the part of the king or lord (or at least a right of qualification: *personae minus gratae*). With the downfall of the Catholic ruling houses these rights largely disappeared. The way was thereby made quite free for that general papal nomination of bishops which had long been prepared and which was not officially enshrined in the new Code of Canon Law (unilaterally proclaimed by Rome in 1918 without any say or even consultation on the part of the bishops and the Church).

The at present unlimited right of the Swiss dioceses of Basel, Chur, and St. Gall (as well as Olmütz) to elect their own bishops remained the great exception. It is only in the Eastern churches linked with Rome that the right to fill the see derived from the early Church has remained partially operative and has recently been written into the new Code of Canon Law for the Eastern churches: As a general rule, the bishop is elected by the synod of bishops of the patriarchate. At the same time the freedom to vote is diluted (an instructive example!) in so far as the list of candidates has to be approved by Rome beforehand!

As It Ought To Be

History makes it quite clear that the great freedom of the right to elect the bishop in Basel is, practically speaking, in the entire Catholic Church today a unique example not only of the greater freedom that prevailed in earlier times but of that which ought to obtain in the line of Vatican II in all dioceses of the Catholic Church.

It goes without saying that this particular way of conducting an election — particularly in regard to the anachronistic cooperation of the organs of state — is not ideal. Nevertheless the electoral procedure of the diocese of Basel is the nearest thing there is to the original and normative conception of the Church as well as to the new order envisaged by Vatican II. It represents an important and seminal growth-point for a possible new regime of episcopal election in the spirit of Vatican II: a reintegration of clergy and laity on the model of the old Church. This is not the place to expound how this is to happen in detail. What we can envisage immediately is an election in the future which involves not only the cathedral chapter but elected representatives of the clergy and laity of the various deaneries. We can also envisage an election operating through a diocesan council composed of clergy and layfolk in accordance with the directives of Vatican II.

10

Women in Church and Society

Fundamental Theological Ideas

1. Beginning with the concept of God, an overemphasis on masculinity must be avoided. God cannot be claimed exclusively for the male sex. "God" is not identical with "man"; in the Old Testament God also has feminine, motherly traits. Calling God "Father" must not signify a sexual differentiation in the deity Itself. God as "Father" is a patriarchal symbol, an analogue for the transhuman, transsexual reality of God, who is also the origin of all that is feminine and motherly. In no case should this symbol be used as a religious justification for a patriarchal social system.

2. The animosity and even hostility of many Church Fathers and subsequent theologians toward women does not reflect the attitude of Jesus but rather the attitude of numerous male contemporaries of Jesus, who thought women were socially insignificant and believed they should avoid the company of men in public. The Gospels, however, in the historical biographical details, do not hesitate to speak of Jesus' relations with women. According to gospel accounts, Jesus disregarded the custom of excluding women from public life. He displayed not only a lack of contempt for women but also a remarkable openness toward them: from the very beginning, women belonged to the special followers of Jesus, who supported him and accompanied him and the twelve disciples from Galilee to Jerusalem. Personal attachment to women was not alien to Jesus; women witnessed his death and burial. When he forbade husbands, who were the only ones allowed to draw up a letter of divorce, to divorce their wives, Jesus raised the human and juridical status of women in his society considerably. Therefore, no Christology may emphasize Jesus' masculinity more than his humanity (as the title "Son of God" seems to do). God's revelation

did not occur specifically through a man but rather through a human being.

3. In a Mariology formulated by celibate men, Mary, the mother of Jesus, a figure whom we can historically comprehend only in vague outline, has been largely robbed of her sexuality. For a long time she has been absolutized as Christianity's only important female figure and has been placed on a par with Christ. Such a cultic veneration of Mary has not, however, affected the estimation of women in the social realm. What is more, as a result, the multiplicity of female figures mentioned in the Bible (from judge and prophetess Deborah and the young woman in the Song of Songs to church leaders Phoebe and the missionary Prisca) has been neglected. Only a Mariology which does not avoid a historical analysis of her virginity and accepts Mary as a complete woman, instead of simply as an exemplary humble handmaid, can help people of today to a better understanding of the Christian message.

Women in Society

4. The subordination of the wife is not intrinsic to a Christian marriage. New Testament statements concerning the subordination of a wife to her husband (mostly found in later New Testament writings) must be understood in their sociocultural context and present sociocultural conditions must be taken into account. Many married couples of today have discovered that a marriage based on equality is in greater accord with the dignity of human beings who, as man and woman, have both been created in the image of God.

5. Nor can one deduce from the essence of a Christian marriage a specific division of labor — for instance, that the woman is to raise the children, while the man is to be the breadwinner. Raising children and doing housework, as well as financially supporting the family, can be performed by wife and husband together.

6. Parents should, therefore, encourage their daughters no less than their sons to get a good academic education or vocational training. By the same token, sons should be trained for future parental and household duties. To be sure, "working women" is not identical with "liberated women," but neither should the opportunities of women be seen exclusively in the alternatives married and housewife or unmarried and religious. In raising one's children, in sermons, religion class, and marital counseling, the multiplicity of occupational opportunities and roles for women should be emphasized.

7. Birth control, if practiced responsibly and not abused to exploit the woman (the sexual revolution is not to be equated with women's

liberation!), can contribute to the genuine liberation of women by making it possible for them to complete their education, better co-ordinate career and family life and — especially where lower-class women are concerned — reduce their financial burden and work-load.

8. In the controversial issue of abortion one must take into account not only the rights of the fetus but also the physical and mental health of the woman, her social situation, and her family responsibilities, particularly in relation to existing children who must be provided and cared for.

Women in the Church

9. In order that the Catholic Church, whose power structure and ministry are completely dominated by men, might become a Church of all human beings, women should be represented in all decision-making bodies and at all levels — the parish, diocesan, national, and international. A blatant example of women's nonrepresentation is the Vatican Congregation for Religious. Not one single woman is a member of this body. Further, according to present legislation, only men can be voting members of an ecumenical council, and only men can elect a pope. These are questions of human, not divine, law.

10. Since liturgical language should express the fact that the congregation is composed of both women and men who have equal rights, one should never address the "brothers" or the "sons of God" only, but also the "sisters" and "daughters of God," or both together as "children of God." Rather than speaking of Christ redeeming "men" or "mankind," one can say "people" or "humanity."

11. Women should be encouraged to study theology. In order that the Church and theology (ethics, and in particular sexual ethics) profit in all aspects from the insights of women, they should be admitted to all degree programs in theology (including those at Catholic seminaries) — in many places they are still admitted only under certain conditions or not at all — and should be supported by church institutions no less than male theology students (through church scholarships, the subsidizing of scholarly works, etc.).

12. Members of women's religious orders that have often been highly effective in realizing Vatican II's principles of reform are often more hindered than helped by the male official church. In spite of the lack of priests, they are seldom allowed to take over leadership functions in congregations, and, although church funds are amply bestowed upon candidates for the priesthood, they are often denied the financial means to an adequate education. A remedy is urgently needed, especially

in view of the rapidly shrinking numbers of women entering religious orders.

13. The forced celibacy of priests often leads to an unnaturally tense relationship between priests and women, in which women are frequently viewed as sexual beings only and a sexual temptation. Thus there is a connection between the prohibition of marriage for ordained men and the prohibition of ordination of women; women will not be ordained and will not be fully accepted as colleagues in the administrative and decision-making bodies of the Church until clerical celibacy is replaced by a celibacy freely chosen by those truly called to it.

14. The reintroduction of the diaconate of women, which was first abolished by the Western Church and then died out in the Eastern Church, would be a desirable reform. But if the admission of women to the diaconate is not accompanied by their admission to the presbyterate, this measure instead of leading to equality will just delay the ordination of women. Further, those Catholic parishes which now allow women to assume some liturgical functions (conducting Mass, serving as lay readers, distributing communion, giving the sermon) are to be highly commended. But while this can be an important step toward the full integration of women into church leadership, it, too, does not render superfluous the full ordination of women.

15. There are no serious theological reasons opposing the presbyterate of women. That the council of the Twelve was exclusively male must be understood in light of the sociocultural situation of the time. The reasons for the exclusion of women offered by tradition (through woman sin entered the world; woman was created second; woman was not made in the image of God; women are not full members of the Church; menstruation makes woman impure) cannot call on Jesus as their witness, and are evidence of a fundamental theological defamation of women. In view of the leadership of women in the early Church (Phoebe, Prisca) and in view of the completely changed status of today's women in the economic system, in academia, state, and society, the admission of women to the presbyterate should be delayed no longer. Jesus and the early Church were ahead of their time in their estimation of women; today's Catholic Church is far behind the times, and also far behind other Christian churches.

16. It would be a misunderstanding of ecumenism if the Catholic Church, referring to the reserve of more conservative "brother churches," were to delay long overdue reforms such as the ordination of women. Instead of using other churches as an alibi, they, in turn, should be challenged to reform. On this issue many Protestant churches could serve as a model for the Catholic Church.

For a long time both in theory and practice, the Catholic Church has discredited and defamed women and at the same time exploited them. Along with the dignity due them, it is time to guarantee women an appropriate juridical and social status.

11

Discussion on the Future
of Pastoral Care

PASTORAL CARE ON THE BRINK OF COLLAPSE:
AN OPEN LETTER TO A PASTOR

Dear Confrere,

Your letter is only one of many; almost daily letters come to me from pastors or religion teachers, committed men and women from our communities, expressing their profound concern over the dramatic emergency facing our Church. But you are right: The open letter (January 1983) of Bishop Dr. Georg Moser to the church councils in the diocese of Rottenburg-Stuttgart on the dramatic situation of pastoral care moved me greatly too. It is a sign that the concern many people share is now slowly beginning to be the cause of the bishops too. A hopeful sign.

A Dramatic Situation

For there is something here deserving acknowledgment: At last a German bishop has openly expressed what all bishops have already known for years. In summary fashion the balance sheet on pastoral care for German Catholics looks like this:

- Many communities no longer have their own pastor and have to "share" a priest with one or more parishes.

- We now have an unbearable situation where on great feast days a priest has to celebrate several services with brief intervals and sees the community only at the altar.

106

- The same holds true for normal Sundays, especially in many larger parishes; it is not unusual for a priest to hold five Eucharists on one weekend.

- In numerous communities there are no full-time pastoral aides available to prepare children and young people for confession and communion.

- Unlike earlier days priests are expected — along with extraordinary tasks — to engage in time-consuming, exhausting individual conversations and advising sessions: for baptisms, marriage, conflict situations, for the sick and dying.

- Many pastors, even some whose health has suffered, have to remain in service past retirement age.

"These items are highlights," the bishop says, "that clarify the situation at some painful points, but nevertheless do not exhaustively describe it." In fact, many of our colleagues can report in heart-rending ways what is demanded of them in the way of physical and mental overburdening. Even before — I know this from personal experience — it was difficult to meet all one's obligations as a priest in a larger parish. But then they usually had one pastor and two curates. Today often enough we find a single pastor without even one curate responsible for several parishes (often more than three). And in each one of what are often very different communities he has to look after liturgy, instruction, the election and functioning of the parish councils, individual pastoral care, and countless other minor duties. This has become unbearable, and the bishop is right: "Who can do that much?"

Yes, you too no longer have a curate. The bishop doesn't even mention curates and vicars, who might lend support to an overtaxed pastor. They have, after all, become a rarity in our dioceses. And the pastors? The case of the Rottenburg diocese is typical — unfortunately.

As early as 1972 the diocesan council in Rottenburg decided that because of the emergency it would set up no more new parishes unless the situation unconditionally demanded it. Nevertheless things keep on going downhill. In 1960 the number of parishes without pastors was 95, by 1978 it had grown to 178, and in 1984 it is expected to surpass 350. The lack of recruits to the priesthood will, however, become still more perceptible when the priests from the large ordination classes leave active service. Given the high average age of priests, the nadir of the vocation shortage will not be reached until the late 1980s and 1990s. Just how quickly things are going downhill here can be shown by a comparison of the number of diocesan priests in service for the year 1979 with the projected figures for 1987: we see a drop from 899 to 512. And the drop for West Germany as a whole is just as dramatic: from 12,165 priests to 7,424 within these eight years.

But even these cheerless figures veil the seriousness of the situation. Because a growing percentage of the clergy in pastoral care are foreigners, and they attend not just to their compatriots but to native Germans as well. In the diocese of Rottenburg it was first the Dutch, then the Croats and Poles. But for all their enthusiasm and dedication, these priests understandably have had linguistic and social difficulties here. There is now a six-man Indian group and a few scattered Africans. I know a deanery in the highland where foreign pastors are already in the majority.

I'm not saying this because we don't owe our foreign brothers all our gratitude for their vital work in our communities, but because I am depressed by the question, Has Germany actually become a missionary country? Are our own intellectual and spiritual forces so exhausted or used up that we will soon become a developing country as far as the Church is concerned? And meantime in other western European countries things are no better: in the last five years the number of diocesan priests in Europe has sunk by around 8,000.

You ask, dear colleague, about the number of candidates for the priesthood, which is now rising again. As you know, the number of ordinations in West Germany has fallen continually from 1964, when it stood at 506, till 1978, when it was 163. Once the numbers have fallen so low, every increase can easily be interpreted as a "turning point." I don't have to tell you how many enter the seminaries but leave before ordination, and — what disturbs some people even more — *which* candidates stay and *which* ones leave. Aren't the ones who leave us often the best?

In any case the prognosis of the German Bishops Conference in their "Perspectives on Medium-Term Personnel Planning for the Dioceses until 1987" remains at once correct and frightening: "We shall not feel the whole burden of the shortage of priests until the next few years. Many communities will no longer have a priest in their midst. Even if the number of the candidates for the priesthood grew by leaps and bounds, this could not bring on a quick turnabout."

I confess to you that this is something that often depresses me greatly: On the official side people see the catastrophe coming, and yet they are incapable of boldly translating into reality any concepts that point toward the future.

The Right Countermeasures?

I can assure you, dear colleague, that the bishop too has been aware of this practically hopeless situation since he was appointed. He too knows all about the numbers and prognoses. What measures does he propose?

- reduction of Sunday masses (more than three eucharistic celebrations on the weekend are too much to ask of a pastor);
- participation of native Germans in services for foreigners and vice versa;
- in parishes without pastors Sunday services without priests (Sunday services with and without priests should alternate);
- agreements between the communities for feast days;
- collective weddings on Saturday afternoon;
- collective funeral services;
- on work days only one worship service per pastor (no separate group services);
- baptisms every four to six weeks;
- use of laypeople as communion helpers, lectors, and leaders of services without priests;
- laypeople as aides for parish catechesis, the preparation of children and young people for confession, first communion, and confirmation; exchange of pastoral aides among the communities;
- an early beginning to parent work, so as to find volunteer aides;
- reduction of the large number of meetings, especially for pastors responsible for several communities and parishes.

What are people among our clergy and our communities likely to say about these measures? The bishop: "Some pastors are afraid of the negative response to such measures." And he himself echoes the typical words of a pastor: "I'm not changing anything. Because if I do, then what I'll get right away is 'First he gives the communion children and the confirmation classes to the group mothers, and now he wants to hold still fewer services.' I'm going on until I drop."

Such remarks have shaken me up, as they should everyone who has a stake in this. In any event I can no longer simply look calmly on this situation. In plain language this means that we are facing the collapse of *pastoral care*. And this is for the Church (not just in Germany) a historical turning point.

I know that it causes you pain too, when you travel through our beautiful country where for a thousand years our forebears have built up a well organized system of pastoral care through infinite sacrifices: every village with a church, every village with a pastor. And now we find more and more orphaned churches, more and more pastors resigning.

The collapse of pastoral care is increasingly accompanied, as the bishop fears, by the *collapse of the providers of that care*. And one should be silent about this, this should be a matter of indifference? No, the tasks of the "cure of souls" are too vital to people for us to go back to business as usual here.

And they have one more justified fear: If after reading the bishop's letter people begin to realize what a tragedy is being played out here and how impotent we are, the question will doubtless be voiced: "Why do we actually pay church *taxes*, if we don't have a pastor any more and are supposed to do everything ourselves on an 'honorary' basis?" "Nevertheless, it can happen," says the bishop, "that one 'sees and yet does not see. . . .' But if we don't react until we're lying flat on the ground, then it's too late." You, my dear colleague, write me on this point: "Bishops themselves see and yet do not see." I can only agree with you: All these emergency measures are unfortunately coming too late and are besides, I believe, *steps in the wrong direction*.

Because the point is not to dismantle pastoral care but to rebuild it. One should not recommend the reduction of liturgical services but their renewal. The idea is not to appoint laypeople as "honorary" substitute priests (aides), but, where appropriate, to ordain them as real priests.

The Consequences of a Reactionary Policy

I myself often wonder: Are we really all struck by blindness, "blind leaders of the blind," as it says in the Gospel? Everywhere in the world there has been an increase (though certainly this is not without its problems) of often creative piety. Only in the Church do we by and large find spiritual paralysis. The well-staged church spectaculars, such as papal visits and Catholic Congresses, only disguise the true condition of our communities: From 1949 to 1980 the percentage of churchgoers in West Germany as a whole fell from 51 percent to 19 percent. The situation is still worse for those under thirty: in the last twenty-five years the number of regular churchgoers has declined (according to the Allensbach Longitudinal Study) from 59 percent to 14 percent. In 1967, 52 percent of all Catholic students regularly went to Mass; by 1982 it was only 13 percent: a 75 percent drop in fifteen years.

You see here the consequences of a progressively glossed over reactionary church policy toward student communities (the German Catholic Student Union, the Association of Catholic University Communities), youth groups, journalists (*Publik*, the *Rheinische Merkur*), religion teachers, theologians, women, and the whole "Church from below," whom they have tried systematically to "discipline" with the tools of canon law (the Concordat) and money. That church policy is now finding drastic expression in red ink, which in any other institution (state, party, trade union, industrial operation) would have led to a radical change in leadership and methods. Fifty-seven percent of German Catholics favor the ordination of women, 67 percent support common Sunday worship for Catholics and Protestants, 71 percent approve remarriage in church for divorced people, 72 percent favor marriage for priests, 74 percent support the removal of marriage impediments based on denominational differences, and 82 percent favor the moral permissibleness of birth control. But the Church's hierarchy draws no consequences from this. It takes its stand on its power and now on its "renewed" Code of Canon Law. The Church, as always, expects other people to change their minds.

Like you, dear colleague, some younger bishops are also, admittedly, beginning to wonder quietly, how can things go on like this? Ever fewer children are being baptized (I read of our sister university of Heidelberg that in recent years over half of the babies eligible for Catholic baptism are not in fact baptized). The Christian socialization of children has become a minority experience. Even though religious instruction has gotten better in many places, the greater part of teenagers and people in their twenties can no longer be gotten into church at all. And now we are to sacrifice the group worship services through which young people might, perhaps for the first time, get some access to the parish Eucharist?

And after a majority of the men have turned their backs on the Church, now a majority of women too are increasingly doing the same — due to the Church's misogynistic position on the issues of birth control, women acolytes, and the ordination of women. This "lack of mothers" has devastating consequences for parish work. And now amid this emergency situation we are going to have still more emergency measures, which will make the emergency worse. Where the need is greatest, God's help seems furthest, because of human blindness. But what, one wonders, would turn the situation around?

The Key Role of Celibacy

Like you, I am convinced that the *prohibition against marriage for priests* plays a fatal part in the catastrophic shortage of priests. This is not because the profound crisis facing the Church could be resolved simply by changes here; but because compulsory celibacy is a test case for a thoroughgoing renewal of the Church's office and church structures in general. For together with the authoritarianism of the Church's hierar-

111

chy (which many pastors too complain about, and which every future priest has to reckon with), the prohibition against marriage is the main reason against entering the service of the Church.

Don't forget that the bishop of Rottenburg was one of the few bishops who dared to speak, at least softly, about this taboo. The subject could not be discussed at the Second Vatican Council, for fear the bishops might change their minds about religious freedom and similar matters. And I know that you are not the only one to complain about this. Under the new pontificate Bishop Moser's critical voice has also been silenced, and in the letter to the parish councils not a word is said about this touchy point.

On this issue the bishop, well educated as he is, would surely agree with us, in private,

- that on the question of marriage Jesus issued no prohibition to his disciples, but allowed them all freedom: "He who is able to receive this, let him receive it" (Matt. 19:12). The same is true of Paul: "Each one has his own special gift from God, one of one kind and one of another" (1 Cor. 7:7);
- that according to the testimony of Paul all the other apostles (including Peter) were married and stayed married;
- that for over a thousand years even in the western Latin Church the scriptural saying held true: "Now a bishop (and a priest!) must be above reproach, the husband of one wife" (1 Tim. 3:2);
- that only in the Middle Ages was the prohibition against marriage for priests imposed on the secular clergy by Rome, sometimes by cruel means;
- that the Eastern Orthodox churches have all kept priestly marriage to this day, and the Reformation churches reintroduced it;
- that Rome allows marriage to the Eastern Uniate churches and to Protestant pastors who convert;
- that this ban on marriage is a law peculiar to the Latin part of the Roman Catholic Church; Catholic theologians agree that it is a purely human law, which could be cancelled overnight.

There is nothing wrong with *freely chosen* celibacy in the spirit of the Bible, but nothing right with an imposed medieval *law of celibacy*. To be sure, the Church's problems would not be solved at a stroke. Still, far more priests would be available for pastoral care if we had kept the ones who have left for this reason and gained those who did not enter in the first place because of celibacy.

Every day we pay more dearly for the fact that we are sinning against the freedom of the gospel, against the original freedom-oriented order of our Church, against the human right to marriage, that we are creating countless conflicts for our pastors and communities — but we don't need to discuss this now. No, *we are not short of priests*. The lack of priests is a pseudo-problem. The office, the responsibility is as attractive, even for young people, as it has seldom been before. The "glut of pastors" in the Protestant churches shows this. *We are short of people willing to be celibates.* But, according to Scripture and the great Catholic tradition celibacy is not at all demanded for the office of pastor (or bishop).

The situation is scandalously paradoxical: Thousands of priests are needed, and yet *there are hundreds of candidates available.* In the Catholic theological faculties of West Germany there are thousands of men and women (in Tübingen alone around one thousand) of which a large part would be willing and able to enter the Church's service. But they have one single "flaw": They would like to get married.

Instead of appealing to these laypeople, we frighten them away from church service by means of control procedures. The numbers admitted as pastoral assistants in German dioceses are deliberately kept low, so as not to get a "laicist" majority in pastoral care. We prefer to let our parishes go under rather than make ordination possible for married lay people. *But our parishes have a right to the Eucharist and to their own pastors*, and they should try to push this agenda by every legitimate means even in the face of opposition from the bishops. For some theological reflections on this question I call your attention to the issue of the international review for theology *Concilium* on "The Community's Right to a Pastor" (vol. 3, March 1980).

In the reactionary Code of Canon Law published in 1983, which scarcely breathes the spirit of John XXIII and Vatican II, the attempt is made, with some cosmetic improvements, to nail down the current legal situation: denying the sacraments to divorced men and women, declaring Protestant orders and eucharistic celebrations invalid, together with banning ordination for women and marriage for priests.

As for the resolutions of Common Synod of Dioceses in the Federal Republic of Germany, which had been worked out over many years and then passed by the bishops, Rome had nothing but disdain for them. Of the nineteen postulates only a single one (in limited form) was actually granted. Nobody bothered about the other eighteen. Do the German bishops at least remember one of the resolutions, which read: "For this reason it is commonly recognized that *extraordinary pastoral emergency situations can require the ordination of men who have been tried in marriage and professional life"*? So are we calling for something that is unfitting or uncatholic?

What to Do?

You ask me, what is concretely to be done? Now the bishop himself asks that his directives be discussed in the parish councils. I would like to advise you and all concerned persons to join in discussing the ideas expressed here, and to debate as well the following genuinely positive measures and to propose *solutions* to the bishop and to the German Bishops Conference:

- In the future no lay theologians should be rejected as pastoral advisors out of the secret fear of a noncelibate majority in the clergy. At a time of unemployment this is also irresponsible from a social point of view.
- All pastoral advisors and deacons who already attend to what are largely priestly duties and who wish ordination may be ordained priests without delay.
- Let all the hundreds of priests who in Germany too have had to give up their priestly vocation just because of the ban on marriage be immediately recalled to their communities. Some of them would answer this call with joy.
- Let our theology students be spared the compulsory choice between priestly service and God-given marriage. Thousands of young people would then be ordained priests.
- Let women no longer be denied ordination — in the light of the biblical message understood in a timely fashion.
- Let freely chosen celibacy in the spirit of the gospel be promoted for special services in the Church.

At the end of your letter, dear colleague, you refer to the fact that during your whole service as a pastor you have continually met Protestant colleagues who precisely as married men fulfill their service to the communities in an excellent manner. The issue of celibacy is also an *obstacle to the reunion of the Christian churches* that should finally be gotten rid of. The Reformation would likely have taken a different course if Rome had immediately granted the justified demands for the vernacular in the liturgy, the chalice for the laity, and marriage for priests. It took 450 years before (at Vatican II) the first two mistakes were acknowledged.

How many priests must we still lose, how many new ones will we not get, before we realize and acknowledge the legitimacy of priestly marriage, with which all other churches have had good experiences? This could be a genuine ecumenical contribution to the 500th anniversary of

Luther's birth (1483), more so than many fine ecumenical words from the mouths of Catholics.

Dear colleague, I am writing this letter to you, not to add my voice to the chorus of general despair, but because despite everything I am confident that we can successfully take the path of church renewal in the spirit of Jesus Christ. The men and women in our communities need you, your courage, your energy, your creativity and inspiration. They need a genuine pastor who gives them some sense of the spirit of Jesus Christ. Always remember that your task as a pastor and counselor is indispensable. And don't resign yourself; that would be a terrible shame for humanity's sake.

I wish you staying power and *inexhaustible hope*. Presumably the waters will have to rise yet more. But many things change more quickly in the world and the Church than people think. Furthermore I remind you of the declaration by thirty-three theologians (six from Tübingen) "Against Resignation" issued a good ten years ago: "One pastor in the diocese doesn't count, five get noticed, fifty are unbeatable."

COLLAPSE OR AWAKENING?
BISHOP MOSER'S ANSWER

Professor Hans Küng of Tübingen has published an article entitled "Pastoral Care on the Brink of Collapse." The notion of pastoral care expressed in it challenges me to respond, above all because Professor Küng composed his remarks as a commentary on my letter of January 1983 to the parish councils of the Rottenburg-Stuttgart diocese.

As a bishop it is not easy to discuss a critique of the Church that has been given a lively presentation in the press. People like myself are immediately under suspicion of wanting to defend everything, even when there is nothing to defend. Nevertheless I do not wish to dodge the task of answering, especially since, along with a series of dialogue partners in recent days, I am of the opinion that the direction that Hans Küng proposes does not make sense. In order to show why I can say that, I have to argue somewhat more pastorally-theologically. But perhaps in today's public climate even a bishop may get a hearing.

The End of the "Provided Parish"

I have no intention of dissociating myself from Professor's Küng's thesis that we find ourselves in a difficult pastoral situation. "Even bishops" have noticed that. The causes of this come from within — and no less from without. In any event traditional pastoral care (whatever one may understand by that) has in fact fallen into a crisis. Around thirty-five years ago a Jesuit priest named Ivo Zeiger was already talking about Germany as a "mission country." Back in those days, at least, the phrase was unusual.

In the meantime there have been many efforts — admittedly still inadequate ones — to deal appropriately and effectively with this extremely varied situation. At the moment we are now having in our diocese the third session of the diocesan council, i.e, the elected authority made up of priests and laypeople. This council has chosen the theme "Proclaiming the Gospel to the Men and Women of Our Time."

All the topics committees of the Council deal with this basic task of the Church. This is the context in which my letter to the parish councils belongs. Here I make suggestions to those in charge of one area of pastoral care for the overcoming of today's crisis. This is what Hans Küng calls "steps in the wrong direction." At this point I would like to raise an objection and offer an alternative to his harsh thesis of the "collapse of pastoral care": In actuality we are facing a collapse — but it is the breakdown of a specific form of pastoral care, that of the "provided parish."

No New Clericalism

Many of us still live with the image of a parish where everything converges on the one man, who because he is ordained has to take charge of all pastoral tasks and responsibilities. The parish fixated on the pastor need only wait to be looked after and provided with everything necessary for the welfare of its body and soul, above all its soul. I don't wish to draw a caricature. Still it seems to me worthwhile to consider which new perspectives of a living community have been opened up to us today. Granted, they have partly grown out of an emergency, specifically from the distressing fact that we no longer have so many priests as before. Still as a believing Christian I count on God's spirit revealing to us both new and forgotten things again in a time of trouble.

Needless to say, such a radical change from the "provided parish" to the "committed community" brings problems and long hauls with it. Still the great opportunity that offers itself to us today and that I refer to in my letter from beginning to end is something Professor Küng just does not see. He finds the momentary situation simply lamentable and can wrest nothing positive from it. I cannot understand why he still conceives of pastoral care exclusively as something given to the laity by ordained priests.

For decades pastoral theology has been trying to define the believing community no longer as an object, but as the subject of pastoral care. A future-oriented concept of the parish has to break with the old idea of providing care. Can the community become autonomous, can questions of pastoral care be answered, can crises be overcome by having as many priests as possible ordained? Can things after that continue to go on as they have before? By this question I do not mean to downplay the problem of the shortage of priests. I only wish to state that we cannot create living communities by paying homage to a new (old) clericalism.

Küng's demand for the ordination of as many people as possible to get out of a difficult faith situation does not reckon with a new self-awareness on the part of the community. If this proposal for a quantitative increase in ordinations — there is no mention of qualitative conditions — were the remedy, then we bishops would logically have nothing to do but to send out enough priests to perform all the services that tax-paying believers make a claim to. But things are not so simple.

A New Understanding of Community

The Church as a service operation designed to cover the territory — this is just the image that has been unequivocally dismissed in various statements by the Church, from the Second Vatican Council to the synods to my letter on the parish councils. Should we now once more turn around on this path because of the seductive opportunity now available of dealing with often heard criticism of the Church? The development has been ongoing. Let me recall some representative instances from official church documents:

- The Council repeatedly (above all in the so-called Constitution on the Church) places the community of believers as God's people ahead of every hierarchy. As opposed to legal incapacitation of the laity emphasis was placed on their participation, based on baptism and confirmation, in the common priesthood (and thus in the saving mission of the Church).

- The joint synod of dioceses in the Federal Republic carries these thoughts further. It does so explicitly above all in the resolution on "Services and Offices." The key sentence and leading idea is here, and it sets the standard as well for the synod's resolutions: "A community that lets itself be taken care of pastorally must evolve into a community that shapes its life in common service of all and in the nontransferable personal responsibility of every individual."

- Continuing this theme in 1981 I submitted the "Guidelines for Pastoral Care" to those responsible for the "cure of souls" in the diocese of Rottenburg-Stuttgart and thereby laid out crucial points for concrete pastoral action. These guidelines start out from the assumption that the Church as a whole and in all its individual actions is a community. I developed this thought of community in three directions: "To believe with one another, to live with one another, to bear witness with one another." This expresses what the Church and parish are by nature and hence should be in practical performance: a community of faith, life, and witness.

• Finally there is the letter, attacked by Professor Küng, to the parish councils. Here I concretized these fundamental considerations for an important section of community life. I deliberately recall the sentence of the synod quoted above and say: "We must all continually convert and confess to this statement."

"The Wrong Direction"?

If I strain the reader here with so many quotations, it is because I want to show him or her that the concept of community sketched out here does not arise from any momentary mood or panic, but has already been carefully thought over and theologically grounded. I decisively reject the hostile comments of Küng, who lays heavy stress on the notion that I am heading in "the wrong direction." I ask him to reconsider his judgment against a pastoral-theological background.

Numbers and statistics that aim to "lay on the table" religious experiences and attitudes have only a limited value as evidence. Nevertheless, in this context I have to answer Küng's presentation with a few numbers. From the following tabulation for the diocese of Rottenburg-Stuttgart an overview can easily be gained:

Number of Catholics	2,100,000
Parishes and other areas of pastoral care	1035
Priests (active)	1048
Regular deacons	88
Pastoral advisors	89
Parish advisors/catechists	520
Priests for the foreign Catholics in the diocese	57
Deacons for the foreign Catholics in the diocese	2

It seems to me that Professor Küng's fixation on ordained priests hinders him from seeing and valuing the broad spectrum of our pastoral services. In any case I acknowledge, for example, our regular deacons as ordained office holders, since I see our pastoral and parish advisors as performing their own kind of church functions and not as a substitute for priests that if we had more priests, it would be better not to have.

"Emergency Measures"?

Earlier, when I sketched the image of a committed community — with autonomous, mature Christians — that was no Utopia. Of course, I too know about parishes of whose vitality I scarcely see any signs, which fill me with great concern, where I wonder and worry: What should I do? But it would not be right to see only the negative, to resign, and to surrender to the mood of catastrophe that Küng now too has kindled. There really has been a host of developments in our community that awaken hope.

When did we ever have so many co-workers? Certainly not in the time before the Council. In the parishes of our diocese twelve thousand parish councillors, together with their pastors, bear the official responsibility for the life of the community. The fact that this service is taken very seriously is evident from participation in elections, which is significantly higher than the number of churchgoers. In addition there are almost five thousand communion helpers, as well as countless leaders of preparation groups for first communion, confession, and confirmation. Professor Küng has obviously not thought of the many individuals active in our advisory groups.

There are, all told, more than twelve thousand laypeople whose services were not in existence "earlier." Their voluntary contributions enable the parishes to learn that they are not consumers but providers of pastoral care. Precisely in communities that have no pastor in place the commitment of these co-workers, especially the parish advisors, is growing. Can one simply label the support and assistance of such developments "mistaken emergency measures"? To me at least it seems out of place to spread a bad mood or even a handful of oversimplifying catchphrases. What we need is sobriety.

Which brings me to what may be Hans Küng's main interest, the parishes that are without priests. How do things actually look? I point to the second statistic cited here:

In the diocese there are:

parishes with no resident pastor	250

of which:

— fewer than 500 Catholics	134
— up to 1,000 Catholics	83
— more than 1,000 Catholics	33

The upshot of this is that if a pastor is responsible for two parishes, then the area of his pastoral care does not as a rule embrace more than three thousand Catholics. If he is responsible for three parishes, then on the average he does not have more than two thousand Catholics to look after. I am the last person to underestimate the burdens that arise from this. I just wonder whether they are heavier than in the diaspora. If Professor Küng is arguing that a pastor "often" bears responsibility for more than three parishes, I can only reply that in our diocese there are no more than three such cases.

What Does "Mission Country" Mean?

But this is not enough. Professor Küng reproaches me for opening up the frontiers long ago for foreign priests. I would like to put myself on the side of these foreign colleagues, because we owe a great deal to their work in this enormous diocese. Sometimes they have a very hard time among us — and sometimes we have a hard time with them — as those involved know perfectly well. But what kind of an understanding for the world Church is in our bones when even widely traveled professors of theology have creeping fears that we could become a "developing country"? Naturally that's what we are, and it's time that we gradually understand that we are not the only ones who can "supply" something to others in matters concerning the gospel.

Küng's Sore Point

Our situation is obviously a difficult one in the most varied directions. But Professor Küng does not make use of these many problems to support impulses for deepening and vivifying faith. Instead he takes my letter to the parishes as an occasion for getting another hearing for his old familiar proposals for reform: above all celibacy and the ordination of women. I don't claim that these serious problem areas are taboo for church discussion, but I do claim that these proposals, in the argumentative context Professor Küng puts them into, are to be rated, theologically speaking, not as progress but as a step backward. Besides, how is Professor Küng so sure that on these issues there is nothing being said "under a new pontificate," that critical voices "fall silent"?

What Is Celibacy For?

It is impossible to give a brief and appropriate presentation of the meaning of priestly celibacy in this article. Still I think that every Christian has already come to terms with the call to follow Christ as it stands in the gospel. For this following of Jesus there are signals designed, as it were, to point out to everyone the alternatives that faith proposes for a more human, God-bound world. One of these is celibacy chosen "for the sake of the Kingdom of Heaven."

When imposed on the priest as a servant of the community, this

120

releases in him new religious and social energies; it can create a new atmosphere of togetherness. Countless believers still know how to appreciate the value of the availability and service that grow out of celibacy for their pastoral care.

To many, however, this form of life, especially as tied into the Church's law of celibacy, is hard to understand. Still everyone who has the bishop lay his hands on him for ordination knows what he is doing. He has given the bishop his reasons beforehand, declaring that he freely accepts the demands of the Church on this score. No one denies that individuals can have problems with this later. But does Professor Küng believe in all seriousness that with the marriage of priests that he so longs for all problems would be solved and no new ones would come upon us?

"Spiritual Paralysis?"

It is my experience that such signals of an open attitude in the face of God and of human beings are very well understood by our rising generation. Some vocations are stifled however, by purely negative criticism. It is by no means the case, as Küng writes, that the "spiritual paralysis of the Church" is perceptible everywhere. Even though statistically proven developments give grounds for hope, I am still suspending my judgment. Nevertheless, the number of participants in retreats and cursillos has more than doubled since 1969. And the number of parish commissions continues to grow. Is that a sign of the collapse of pastoral care?

When I see that and write it here, this does not mean that I cherish any illusions. I also see many depressing things; I see that we have no grounds for triumphal self-incensing. Still in gloomy hours my eyes too have been opened, and I see how much of genuine life is stirring: the many new hymns for example; the very personal intercessory prayers in group liturgies (about which, by the way, I write with an altogether different accent from the one Professor Küng relates in his article); the youth and family encounters, and also the burgeoning powers of groups that one day will resemble the model of some base communities on other continents — to mention only a few key items.

No Collectivity

I would be glad to go further into some points that Hans Küng raises. On the list of topics that disturbed me in the Küng article there is, however, one in particular that I wish to address. It concerns his suggestive, downright demagogic use of the word "collective."

Who likes this sort of thing? Now the Church too is to have "collective weddings," "collective funerals," "collective baptisms." For all three of the events thus described my letter uses the word "in common." Sacraments have their place in the community of the believers. They are not private arrangements for loners. If we are just now in the long process of recognizing the Church once again as God's people, then the community of the sisters and brothers who receive the sacraments as a sign of salvation is not a collectivity. How long will it take us before we improve upon the narrowly individualistic notion of the sacraments in the mind of believers, when we still have to argue about these things even with professors of theology?

The basic questions about pastoral care under discussion here are important and pressing. As before I will go on discussing them with the priests and laypeople of our diocese. There is no doubt in my mind that we have to help one another, even with criticism, if we wish to come close to the goal set up for us by God. Nevertheless, "Let all things be done for edification" (1 Cor. 14:26).

A PASTOR FOR A RESPONSIBLE COMMUNITY: REPLY

It would have been more comfortable to keep silence on this matter. But the reaction of the bishop of Rottenburg-Stuttgart to my open letter to a colleague and the many reactions from the clergy and laity show how important it is to speak. I am doing so not to carry on an endless public debate with the bishop (after all, my letter was not addressed to him), but once again to focus on its subject, which was rather downplayed in the bishop's letter. So now I am taking a public position for a second time, in the interest of the men and women in our communities affected by this.

Common Ground

First of all, we have to be thankful to the bishop that he takes such a vehement stand for the "committed community," for its adult status and autonomy, that he no longer understands the parish as an "object," but as a "subject of pastoral care." And we are grateful to him for the clearcut words on the matter of deacons and pastoral and parish advisors "as performing their own kind of church services, and not as a substitute for priests that if we had more priests we would be better off not having."

In general, the bishop's answer contains a great deal that we can only agree with, if we are concerned about the same human person in the same parishes of this diocese. So as not to be misunderstood again after this, I wish to underline plainly this much:

1. The bishop has not distanced himself from my thesis, "that we find ourselves in a difficult pastoral situation." On the contrary, he too

is of the opinion that we "actually [stand] on the brink of a collapse" of pastoral care, of the "provided parish."

2. Like the bishop I believe that there is no going back nowadays to a traditional understanding of a parish that sees itself as the object of pastoral care (exclusively given by ordained priests), as opposed to itself helping to shape that care. There is likewise no going back to a "service operation that covers the territory," nor to a "narrowly individualistic notion of the sacraments." Rather we must go "forward" to a Church that is not only called "God's people," but is also allowed to live and act like God's people.

3. Along with the bishop I am glad about the thousands of laypeople who are committing themselves as volunteers in our parishes. They are the only ones who are still holding something like parish life upright, and we would find still more of them (or lose fewer), if the official Church had a different attitude toward the question of women.

4. Along with the bishop I am glad that in the Church there is an alternative religious life going on, specifically among young people, in other places than in the traditional parish. The bishop himself mentions retreats, cursillos. I would add: church congresses, base communities, student communities, the whole "church initiative from below." Who would have denied all this?

In Rottenburg they knew, of course, that all this wasn't unknown to me and needn't have been cited against me. Was that why it was necessary, instead of stressing the large amount of common ground in my objective, once again to use unfair means to discredit someone who did not create the problems, but just openly named them? Was it necessary to blame me for seeing "only the negative," for stirring up an "atmosphere of catastrophe," for creating a "bad mood," for spreading around a "pair of simplistic magic formulas"?

Indeed, was it necessary to insinuate that "such purely negative criticism" also stifled "many vocations," after my "Letter to a Colleague" from start to finish had the opposite purpose in mind?

No, all of this would not have been necessary with the "sober" consideration that the bishop is so concerned about and would have spared me a great deal of necessary self-defense. And it most certainly was not necessary to take sides so emphatically "with the foreign brethren." This is a way, admittedly, for leading a popular attack against the "widely traveled professor of theology," but in reality it only shows that the bishop has not read my letter carefully enough. For in it one will find not one word against these brethren, but on the contrary a word of thanks, bound up with a critical question aimed at the *German* church, a question that cannot be gotten rid of just because it was first raised (under the heading of Germany as a mission country) thirty-five years before under essentially different and more favorable conditions: "But does Professor Küng believe in all seriousness that with the marriage of priests that he so yearns for all problems would be solved and no new ones would come upon us?"

Once again there has been sloppy reading: In my letter the problem of celibacy was adjudged to have an unfortunate key role in the catastrophic *shortage of priests* (which nobody seriously denies). And the text clearly reads: "Not because the profound crisis of the Church could be resolved by this alone...."

How Things Really Stand

No, we cannot spare this response from Rottenburg the reproach that on the decisive point it *obscures the true state of affairs*. Even the statistics supplied conceal more than they reveal. Why is it hidden from the public that

- of the roughly 1,000 active priests (for about 1,000 parishes) some 250 are not doing parish work at all;
- besides the 250 parishes without a pastor there are currently about 30 unoccupied parishes;
- the number of parishes without pastors, according to the calculations of the bishop's own diocesan authorities, will rise in the next few years to around 360 parishes?[1]

In the future therefore around *one-third of the parishes will be without a resident pastor. And how are things with the other two-thirds?* Let's not fool ourselves: a large percentage of the pastors is overtaxed, overburdened, and superannuated. This means they scarcely have any time

---

[1]A frightening confirmation of this trend on the national level was provided this year by the Catholic newspaper *Weltbild* (March 23, 1989). The paper entitled an article on the Church in the year 2,000 "Parish without Priests" and agreed with my analysis, down to its choice of words: "The shortage of priests in the Catholic Church has come to a critical head. For a long time now the vacant places can no longer all be filled." According to this article,

1. Since 1965 the number of priests in the twenty-two dioceses of West Germany has continually gone down and at an accelerated pace: from 20, 204 to 15,124 at the end of 1988.

2. The losses in the parishes have been still heavier. In 1950 14,600 priests were active in the pastoral ministry. By 1970 the number had sunk to 12,985; by 1979 to 10,533. Around the end of last year it reached a record low of 9,284.

3. For six years now the number of theology students who wish to become priests has also been steadily decreasing, from 823 in 1983 to only 655 in 1987.

4. The gaps in the German clergy made by priests who retire or die have long since ceased to be repairable by the next generation of priests, but only now are these gaps taking on dramatic proportions.

left over for individual or youth counselling. Many pastors are on the verge of retirement age; most have no curates or assistants. A very large number of pastors will no longer come from the diocesan clergy, but from religious orders. They will no longer come from their own country, but from all over the world. And this with parishes so large (and such long distances to cover) that one can scarcely get an overview of them.

Among the priests themselves there is the feeling of being in a rat-race, of dissatisfaction, of being drained and abandoned. There are unacceptably long delays in assigning new pastors and increasing difficulties in looking for replacements during sickness and vacations. Even for foreign pastors (Italians, Spaniards, and Portuguese) one hears that in the future priests will be scarcely obtainable because of the shortage of priests in those countries.

And now the remaining pastors are supposed to look for still more volunteer personnel to "cover" (despite their being hopelessly over-worked, of course) for all the orphaned parishes. These people will enjoy the confidence of the parishes without pastors and are to serve as "land-ing places" and "dialogue partners. . . . " Actually, why isn't this openly presented to the public when the statistics are cranked out? And how much longer will it take before in the face of the admitted "breakdown of traditional pastoral care " — which wasn't so bad — we dare to speak up publicly for alternative solutions instead of keeping them at arm's length by referring to an "outdated notion of community"?

Unprovided For

Which leads us to the main point: the new *understanding of community*, which Bishop Moser takes as his foundation in opposing my putative "fixation on ordained priests." And here the argument becomes not only sloppy but downright grotesque. The Constitution on the Church from Vatican II is cited with all emphasis against me, of all people, as if they didn't know in Rottenburg that the passages in this Constitution both about the Eastern Church and the various charisms, gifts of grace, and vocations in the Church, and certainly those about the sinful Church, go back to my own drafts as a *peritus* at the Council. As if people did not know that in all my publications I have continually given theolog-ical grounding to the ideal of the "autonomous community" and have developed it in its practical consequences all the way to the election of pastors by the parish community. So I am *toto caelo* removed from the old "servicing mentality," not to mention the old "clericalism."

It is really astonishing to see how in a Church that was and is fixated on the ordained hierarchy of bishops, priests, and deacons (because all this too is found in the Constitution on the Church) and that has allowed a deep chasm to yawn between clergy and laity, the term "provided parish" is suddenly used derogatorily. If there were an *unprovided hospital* would anyone respond to the demand for the hiring of qualified doctors by protesting that it was finally time to say goodbye to the "servicing mentality"? Would anyone say that because there were so many "aides" and that precisely because of the emergency caused by the lack of doctors "new perspectives" and a "new host of developments" had become visible? Shall we praise the hospital serviced by laypeople?

In the Church a similar line of argument has evidently become possible. There are hundreds of parishes without pastors and chaplains — in other words, *unprovided-for communities*. And then the bishop responds to the demand for installing ordained priests in them by saying that this is the servicing mentality and a relapse into clericalism. He maintains that there are after all so many "volunteer aides" on hand, and that it is precisely the crisis caused by the shortage of priests that has brought "new perspectives" and a "new host of developments" into view.

To be sure, our parishes are (fortunately) not hospitals, and our priests not doctors. But one point holds in this case as well as in the other: In our situation, for all the admirable dedication of volunteer co-workers, we cannot seriously dispense with professionally trained individuals who can work full-time. That cannot have been what the bishop of Rottenburg meant by the "new self-awareness of the community," especially since according to Catholic teaching (as I have hitherto understood it) the Eucharist, which after all counts as the center of the Christian community, cannot be validly celebrated without ordained ministers. And who baptizes, marries, buries, and dispenses the other sacraments in our parishes?

Here the serious question is raised: Has it not always been the foremost responsibility, or rather the *holy duty of a bishop* — more important than his confirmation trips, his representative and administrative activities — *to see to it that the Lord's Supper can be celebrated in a parish?* After centuries of building up pastoral care in our country could anyone have dreamed that the German bishops and even this diocese would have to set up committees in order to organize "Sunday worship without priests"?

Is it "clericalism" when we demand a pastor for communities without one? When we truly do this not to deprive the parish of its adult status but so as once more to make possible an authentic sacramental life for the parish and an appropriate kind of preaching so that the communities may not become dependent on a traveling "maintenance priest"?

I can't believe my ears: As a Catholic theologian I ask for something archetypically Catholic from a Catholic bishop: *one pastor for one respon-*

sible community. And in exchange I get accused of conceiving pastoral care merely as "looking after the laity with ordained priests" and seeking a purely "quantitative increase in the ordination of priests." If that is clericalism, then I gladly concede that I am more clerical than the clerical hierarchy.

But who is really standing up for the "old clericalism"? The one who calls for ordered pastoral arrangements in the parishes while asking for theologically trained laypeople as pastorally appropriate community leaders? Or the one who is glad to draw upon laypeople for auxiliary services but in the final analysis denies them the corresponding responsibility and competence to decide, the one who refuses to ordain hundreds of capable pastoral advisors as priests because they are married, who prefers parishes without pastors instead of questioning the ban on marriage for priests?

Realism — Not Pessimism

I know that the Church's goal today must be to give fresh encouragement to young people to serve the Church, and I have continually done so. But this can't be done honestly unless one realistically describes the way things are in our communities and at the same time sketches out and tries to implement concepts that can reverse that reality. But we must wonder whether the bishop's answer reflects the real situation in our parishes, especially in those that have already been suffering for years from the lack of priests. It should not be construed as self-boosterism, but as a contribution to realism (not to be confused with pessimism or a mood of catastrophism), if I quote a few sentences from a letter written to me by a pastor from this diocese: "You express what many Christians, laypeople and priests, are thinking. The latter, in their resignation, often have no more strength for it. They just muddle on. In most cases they have only a few more years to go. Why should they put their back into it? They'd rather spare their nerves."

Many reactions, oral and written, take the same approach. In a community where the pastor, after reading out the bishop's pastoral letter, said that he fully supported my challenge to bring the married priests back into the parishes, there was spontaneous, prolonged applause in the church. Isn't he right to say, "The bishops have no idea, or they simply don't want to believe what the rank and file think..."?

Such lines are distress signals. They don't aim to create a split between bishop and priests, or bishop and theologians, but they encourage a common struggle. How are we to move on in our Church? The bishop rightly reminds us that, "as a believing Christian," he takes into account the fact "that in emergency situations God's Spirit once again lets us recognize both new and forgotten things." I too am deeply convinced of this. Hence all my alternative suggestions have the common feature of bringing to light *forgotten things from the earliest Catholic tradition* in the current crisis facing the Church.

In this way I aim to discover a Catholic past that could once again become our Catholic future. Why does the bishop sweep them aside as "old familiar suggestions for reform"? Have we gotten so far in our Church that suggestions aren't taken seriously just because they have been offered for years or presented by a certain theologian? Why doesn't the bishop say a word about the notion he (and the German Synod too) once defended, namely that "proved married men" should be ordained?

Why is there not a single substantial reason given for rejecting the suggestion of ordaining suitable pastoral advisors, men and women, as priests, and recalling priests who have been dismissed only for getting married? Why is there no mention of the ban on the ordination of women, nothing about lay theologians, who would be available for priestly service and who are coming to the Church in great numbers in the next few years? At the moment there are thirteen thousand Catholic students of theology at German universities: What is to become of them (in an age of academic unemployment)?

And doesn't the bishop's brief defense of celibacy miss the actual problems? I raised no doubts about the voluntariness of priestly celibacy, nor about the fact that "countless believers still appreciate deeply the value of the service and availability of the priest, which grow out of celibacy." On the contrary, I myself said that freely chosen celibacy deserves to be promoted in the Church, especially for certain time-consuming and mobile tasks.

But *may celibacy be made a law for all priests on the basis of the gospel?* That is the question for which the bishop has no answer.

And a final point: I too don't like the word "collective," but isn't it a kind of "collectivism" when we demand that members of the community, for organizational reasons stemming from the shortage of priests, share the most personal church services such as marriages and funerals with other people, who perhaps come from a completely different situation? This is less the question of a "narrowly individualistic notion of the sacraments" (which I, like the bishop, reject) and more a question of pastoral style.

Indeed I too see the "great opportunity that is offered to us today." I too find the situation this moment not simply "lamentable." I too can gain from it "something positive": I think that the Church has new opportunities if it makes use of them decisively and with an eye for the true realities.

One should not always — out of a churchly-bureaucratic rationale — dismiss the little village parishes as irrelevant. Even the little parish, if one lets it stay as such, has the right to a pastor. For what kind of an opportunity would it mean for smaller rural parishes (as for suburban ones) whose mayor and school have been taken away, if they were at least allowed to keep a pastor and a spiritual-cultural center? What kind of an opportunity would it mean if right now youth counseling, which has perhaps suffered the most from the lack of priests, could once again be intensified? Many laypeople up and down the country will back me up on this: A parish can function all by itself only with difficulty, but where it has a good pastor, then there is also a good common life. From a pastoral point of view, therefore, we should strive rather to divide up large parishes than to lump together small ones.

It has not yet been decided which concept will prove the most serviceable for the Church of the future. One thing is certain: The question of what is happening to our communities, to the religious life in our cities and villages, to the catechesis of children and young people, will not be dealt with quickly. This is because — as the bishops themselves tell us — we will reach the high point of the priest shortage only in the beginning of the 1990s. In order to overcome the current severe crisis, we need a new collaboration, resting on trust and critical loyalty, involving everyone in the Church, not least of all bishops and theologians — in the interest of the men and women concerned.

Postscript, November 20, 1989

My worst fears have been confirmed by Bishop Moser's successor, Dr. Walter Kasper: Around the year 2000, according to estimates from the diocese of Rottenburg-Stuttgart, there will be 25 percent fewer pastors. On the same day *Time* magazine published the estimate of American experts that in the year 2000 the 54 million Catholics will have only around half as many active priests as there were in 1965 for 46 million. While in Germany there is talk, remarkably, of a "new opportunity," American bishops are deeply disturbed by these "substitute services" without priests ("Why," they say, "can't we ordain other people rather than just celibate men?"[2])

---

[2]Just how dramatic the situation is in Latin America, Africa, and Asia, too, is documented with the figures cited in *Pro Mundi Vita* — Studies, no. 12, November 1989: "Gemeinden ohne Pfarrer am Ort."

12

Worship Today — Why?

Can We Speak to God?

The Alternative

Some years ago Rudolf Augstein, editor of *Der Spiegel*, captured public attention with a theological book, *Jesus Menschensohn* (Jesus, Son of Man).

The theologians criticized this book from top to bottom — unfortunately, not without reason. The last chapter however deserves serious consideration. It represents the climax of the whole book: "Without him what is to be done?" What is to be done without Jesus Christ?

Augstein's clear alternative to Christian faith is: "There is no God whom we know or about whom we can speak" (p. 408). We must "live without religion" (p. 422). We are not spared the necessity "of leaning out into nothingness" (p. 423). Of course we have to "survive" (p. 423). But how? By "applying our reason to the thoroughly banal process of coping with life" (p. 425). We must simply attempt to "make the best we can of ourselves, our life and society . . . in meaningful work, meaningful joy, meaningful hate" (p. 425). "If we improve nothing, if we fail, then we are at least no worse off than before" (p. 426).

This then is the alternative to Christian belief in God. I respect it and I do not want to belittle any of it. Atheists often lead better lives than Christians. Nevertheless I must raise some questions:

Should we — even nonreligious parents often ask themselves this question — educate our children and the younger generation as a whole, without faith, for the rational, banal process of coping with life: without a final orientation, without deeper meaning, higher ideals, without great and living hope?

Should they then have no other support than themselves and their easily deceived, confused, seduced reason? Exposed to all the addictions, constraints, and ideologies of our time?

Can we then give them no answer to those questions of human life which cannot be suppressed simply by prohibiting them? Where do we come from and where do we go to?

Why do what we do? Why is the world as it is?

Why are we here? What is it all about?

What then is the ultimate reason and meaning of all reality?

And what really holds for our action: Why and to whom are we ultimately responsible? What deserves contempt and what love?

Why fight at all for justice and freedom?

What is the point of loyalty and friendship, but also what is the point of suffering and guilt?

And finally what is there left for us: death, making everything point-less at the end? What will give us courage to live and courage to die?

In all these questions it is all or nothing. They are questions not for weaklings and uninformed people but precisely for the informed and committed. They are not excuses for not acting but incentives to action.

Is there something which sustains us in all this, which never permits us to despair?

Something stable in all change, something unconditioned and abso-lute in the relativizing experienced everywhere?

And what is the character of this ultimate reality? Good or evil? In-different or friendly to human beings? Incomprehensible, without any qualities, or perhaps even greater than all that can be conceived?

I think that Christian faith has answers to all these questions and they are not cheap answers. There are of course cheap Christian answers. But today particularly, as Christians, we do not have to believe every absurdity. For there is a midway between unbelief and superstition.

It is that utterly reasonable and yet more than reasonable reliance on an ultimate great mystery in our life which demands trust, requires a commitment, and which at the same time makes it possible both to stand still and to go forward.

Everyone believes in something. Rudolf Augstein believes in human reason. After many experiences of recent, very recent history, I prefer to believe in God: as a wholly rational human being, I think, to believe in God.

Believing in God

There is an alternative to the unbelieving, purely rational, thoroughly banal affirmation of life which is once more being actively propagated today. It is to believe in God and not in human reason, but to do so as a wholly rational being.

What does this mean? It is true that we can no longer believe like ancient and medieval people in a God who dwells literally or spatially "above" the world, from whom the Son of God "descends" and to whom he again "ascends": These are images, profound images, symbols. Nor can we any longer believe in a God who dwells in the intellectual, metaphysical sense "outside" the world in an extramundane beyond and who only occasionally intervenes in this world.

No, a modern understanding of God must explain how God is *in* this world and this world in God: a God who eludes our apprehension and comprehension as air or light elude us when we want to grasp them and who nevertheless is more real than all that is real: the ultimate reality in human hearts and at the heart of things; the infinite in all the finite, the constant in all the inconstant, the unconditioned, the absolute in all that is conditioned and relative; the unfathomable, inscrutable primal reason, primal source, primal meaning of all that is. We must start out from this.

If then I had to say quite simply why we do not have to fear this primal reason, as a Christian, I would point to this Christ. In the man Jesus of Nazareth it has become unambiguously clear that this primal reason of the world and of humankind is not a dark and awful chasm but a superradiant, loving expanse of light, behind all the clouds, on whom we can absolutely rely on clear days or dark days, in living and dying.

God as revealed in Jesus is the guarantee, not only that all will be well at the end but that everything has meaning here and now: that there is meaning in living, loving, acting, in committing ourselves to justice, freedom, human dignity; that there is also meaning in despising some things and respecting others, in keeping faith, cultivating friendship, but also in forgiving sin and enduring suffering.

We should reflect more on what joy God means, could mean, for human life and remember that it was precisely this Jesus who made people aware of the fact. So we have every reason to be grateful.

Thanking

From time to time — and the act of worship provides an opportunity for this — we should at least take a couple of minutes to think of what lies behind us. There is much that we do not want to recall. But there is much that we simply cannot recall without giving thanks. For "thanking" and "thinking" are originally the same word.

What do I want to give thanks for?

Well, certainly for all that is taken for granted, but which so many cannot take for granted: for health, food and drink, clothes, holidays, so many joys. But also for all developments for the better in human society: progress in science and technology, social progress, improvement in international relations. . . .

But everyone has also quite personal reasons for gratitude. For instance, I wrote a dangerous theological book and I have come safely through another year; I went skiing and did not break my leg; I drove a car and was lucky.

And there are other small miracles: colleagues who were never dishonest; reconciliation after a serious quarrel; friendship which has endured; help when help seemed impossible; a way out of a hopeless situation.

So then I would like to give thanks. To whom? Well, to *all* those to whom I owe so much.

Often, admittedly, it was sheer chance that all went well. But we cannot thank chance. As a believer, I would like to thank the one who stands behind chance, who is at work in all things, to whom I owe myself.

You may perhaps ask: Can we speak to God? Is God a person? Well, certainly not a person like you and me: the primal reason and primal meaning of all reality is not an individual person alongside other persons. But God is certainly not less than a person. God is not impersonal.

Or could a God without mind and understanding be a God? Could such a God explain mind and understanding, freedom and love, in the world and in human beings? No, God is not below our level.

Even though we can speak of God only in analogical terms, in metaphors and images, nevertheless we can speak to God. From the first page to the last the Bible speaks of a genuine partner, who loves people and is absolutely reliable: not an object, not empty, unechoing space, not an anonymous interpersonal something, but a genuine Thou.

I want then to thank this God and trust myself to God continually for the future. Sometimes I find help in a prayer that a young Jew, if I remember rightly, wrote on the wall of the Warsaw ghetto, a very encouraging, cheering prayer:

> I believe in the sun, even if it does not shine.
> I believe in love, even if I do not feel it.
> I believe in God, even if I do not see him.

In joy and pain, happiness and unhappiness, we may speak to God. This is our great opportunity, a true grace, the grace of God. Here is the ground of all prayer and all worship.

But what does worship, religious service, mean? Is worship only for Sunday?

Worship in Ordinary Life

Paul writes to the community in Rome:

> I exhort you therefore, brothers, by the mercy of God, to offer your
> bodies as a living sacrifice, holy and pleasing to God. This is your
> spiritual service of God. Do not be conformed to the structure of
> this world, but be transformed in a new mind, so as to be able to
> test what is God's will, that is what is good, pleasing, and perfect.
>
> (Rom. 12:1–2)

The Church today is not always a pleasant sight. But at least one
aspect is pleasing. Both Catholics and Protestants have gained a new
awareness of the fact that the Christian religious service cannot be restricted to congregational worship on Sundays. Their divine service is,
should be, can be essentially service of God in the midst of the world,
in the midst of human society, in the midst of their wholly personal
daily life. Genuinely Christian worship consists in being a Christian in
ordinary life. This is how the Christian praises and honors God.

This is just what is meant by these two programmatic statements
placed as a leitmotif as the opening of the most detailed exhortation
(parenesis) which the Apostle Paul ever wrote. In this letter to the community in Rome he appeals to God's mercy, not insisting on a burden-
some duty or obligation but pointing to a great opportunity, a decisive
possibility, a true grace for human beings. For Christian worship must be
something quite different from the sacrifices which people have offered
in the course of the history of religions from the most ancient times:

- not a sacrifice of slaughtered animals or the offering of dead, material
  things but the living commitment of human beings themselves, in
  unobtrusive service to others, sympathetic or unsympathetic, who
  are living with them and around them. This then is worship of God:

- not only on certain holy days, Sundays, and feast days but on all days,
  on working days throughout the year;

- not only at certain sacred places but in all places — even the most
  profane — in the world;

- not only in the form of certain sacred actions but in our whole life,
  work, struggle, suffering;

- not offered only by certain sacred persons but by all kinds of believing
  Christians.

This is worship therefore which is not — so to speak — interiorized
as a private refinement of our personal existence but which is also a

practical, public gesture on a large or small scale; worship which is not only devout and edifying for the soul but for the whole person with flesh and blood, mind and body, brain and sexuality: "Offer your bodies as a living sacrifice, holy and pleasing to God."

It is clear that this is not what is usually described as "worship." But that very thing which appears to be completely secular, profane, is described by the apostle as "holy" and "pleasing to God": a "spiritual service" which is not tied to outward ceremonies, to particular times, places, or persons, but which takes place in the Spirit, in accordance with what John says, "in spirit and in truth" (John 4:23).

Worship on Sunday?

That much had to be said directly in the light of Paul's text. But I don't want to make it too easy for myself. Anyone in our churches today who wants to be open-minded and to speak frankly in a way suited to the times will also have to speak of the worldliness, secularity, profanity, and rationality of the Christian life. But, where so many are already loudly playing the same tune, we need not blow our own trumpet. Here we shall consider the facts and — in order not to be too boring — try to add a counterpoint.

It must be recognized that the situation today is completely different from that in which Paul made his statement. What Paul could take for granted in his exhortation to offer God our service in ordinary life has largely disappeared. He was writing to a congregation: quite concretely, to a congregational assembly where the letter was read aloud. Could Paul ever have imagined that he would one day be writing for Christians most of whom no longer assemble at all for a religious service, for prayers or the Eucharist in the congregational gathering — even in a very secular place? I am not thinking simply of those Protestant churches which are almost empty on Sundays. In West Germany attendance in the Catholic Church on Sundays has also seriously declined: from 50.6 percent in 1950 to 32.4 percent in 1972. Against these reduced numbers in the shrunken congregations must be set the figure of 84 percent of Christians in the same area who, according to a survey, did not want to leave the Church. But what is particularly disturbing is the fact — to which many pastors can testify — that young people between sixteen and twenty-five scarcely count among churchgoers. In view of these conditions, what will the situation be like in a few decades?

In the light of this alarming state of affairs in Protestantism and Catholicism, unfortunately not only in Germany, I shall make bold — and I am well aware of the risk involved — to speak now not about worship in ordinary life but about worship on Sundays in church. Is this permissible, particularly for a Catholic speaking in a Protestant church? Certainly, according to Martin Luther. In his Larger Catechism he requires participation in Sunday worship precisely in the name of the freedom of a Christian and vehemently attacks the indolence of those "loathsome spirits . . . who, after hearing a sermon or two, have had enough and more than enough, and think they can get on very well by themselves and have no need of a master" (third commandment): merely "celebrating and being idle" does not make a "Christian's feast day"; non-Christians could do as much. Similarly, according to the Reformed Heidelberg Catechism, "particularly on feast days God's congregation should come diligently to learn the Word of God, to make use of the holy sacraments, publicly to invoke the Lord and to give Christian alms" (Question 103). Calvin supported the commandment with the aid of disciplinary and police power. But this is something which I would certainly not recommend.

One thing, however, should be clear. No one who tries to play off against each other religious service in ordinary life and religious service as a special assembly of the congregation can appeal to Paul. On the contrary, Paul took for granted the congregational service and wrote about it only when — as in Corinth — there were conflicts. So I feel particularly encouraged here by Paul, who issues a strong warning against acclimatization and adaptation — literally "conformism" — to the trends prevailing in the world. Paul appeals to critical judgment, to reason, which of course needs renewal, precisely in order to test and distinguish in every situation and — when necessary — to dissociate oneself and to do so according to the supreme norm of the will of God, who wants what is good, pleasing, and perfect: "Do not be conformed to the structure of this world, but be transformed in a new mind, so as to be able to test what is God's will, that is what is good, pleasing, and perfect."

Crisis of Worship — Crisis of the Church

In this notorious crisis there is, of course, no simple and easy formula which avoids conformism while providing a positive justification of Sunday worship. Certainly the crisis is to a large extent the result of *developments in society* as a whole. Some things are clear.

In the drift to secularization and industrialization the former homogeneous society, under definite religious influences, has been largely dissolved. The influence of the churches in the political, economic, educational, and social fields has been restrained. Religious life and activity have long ceased to be taken for granted. Social pressure to attend church — apart from conditions in relatively compact Catholic villages and small towns — has in practice wholly disappeared. Sunday attendance at a religious service, formerly taken for granted, has become a private affair. Thus what was known as the Church of the people, the traditional Church, has been increasingly replaced by a Church of decision, demanding from each individual a personal reaction, a free decision of faith, and a free practice of faith. A numerical decline is understandable in these conditions, but it is only partly compensated by more deliberate and more decided faith.

Many, who acknowledge God and Jesus Christ in practical life, cannot make up their minds to attend a religious service regularly. And this fact alone shows that it is not merely the "wicked world" or secular society, unwilling to accept an invitation to a religious service, which is responsible for the crisis of worship. The very *churches* which invite people to come and worship are also responsible.

The reason is that they themselves appear so uninviting to many of our contemporaries — even our Christian contemporaries — so inhospitable, inhuman, and even un-Christian.

As an example of a church which must seem uninviting, I suggest the Catholic Church in West Germany, with which I am more familiar (there are certainly other examples). There we had a synod recently which closed after meeting over a number of years. The synod drew up a modern-sounding, wordy document on our hope, but never once took any bold step in response to the hopes which many in Germany and elsewhere had set on it. It did not offer

- hope for married people tormented by their conscience, who were expecting at least an unqualified approval of "artificial" birth control and a dissociation from the encyclical *Humanae Vitae*;

- hope for divorced people who want to take part again in the eucharistic celebration;

- hope for students of theology who feel called to parish ministry but not to celibacy (in the course of only three years from 1969 to 1972 there was a decline of about 60,000 candidates for the priesthood in the Catholic Church);

- hope for priests who had to give up their ministry because of a legitimate marriage, many of whom would like to be called (this has meant a loss of more than 30,000 priests in the last ten years in the world as a whole and even now — according to information from Rome — an annual loss of 3,500 to 4,000 priests);

- hope for parishes deprived of their priests to a rapidly increasing extent and having to make do with laypersons authorized to give Holy Communion, largely as a result of the law of celibacy, which is clearly contrary to human rights, expressly contradicts the words of Jesus and

137

Paul, and goes against a practice maintained in the Catholic Church as a whole for its first thousand years;

- hope for responsible people, priest and laity, in the dioceses, who expect to have some say in the choice of their bishops and are looking for a more democratic procedure to secure this (to say nothing of papal elections);

- hope for all the people and the congregations in the different churches who want at last mutual recognition of church ministries and an open eucharistic fellowship, common building and common use of churches, and so on.

I hope that what I have said will not be taken in the wrong way and I would not like to give the impression that I am running down the synod. So many men and women boldly committed themselves and wanted to achieve so much more. But the majority of the bishops did not want more, because — and this is an open secret — Rome does not want more. Thus priests and parishes affected will be provoked to take measures to help themselves and thus unfortunately to further uncontrolled experiments, disorder, and polarization. But again we must ask: Is such a Church, talking so much about hope and doing so little to create it, likely to be effective in inviting people to its services? Is it not this unsympathetic, immobile, senile, blind institutional Church under which also many loyal churchgoers themselves suffer? Is it surprising if congregations are becoming smaller in such a Church, where claim and reality, talk and action, diverge so scandalously?

In view of this situation in society and Church, it is not easy to answer the question: "Worship today — why?" And I would not want to give the impression that one person had to answer this question on behalf of all the rest. It is for every serious Christian to begin again to consider thoroughly the question of the religious service. Here then are some ideas to provoke further reflection, at the same time assuming that today fulfillment of a commandment, consideration for the family, habit, and the need of fellowship no longer provide adequate motivation for attending a religious service. I would like to invite you to reflect on the opportunity which a religious service can offer even today: first for the individual, then for the community. Here then is a first, brief consideration.

For People's Sake

Politicians and directors of industry, even scholars and busy people in all callings, in the midst of constant strain and stress, complain that they are unable to find time for reflection, to ask what is the point of it all, what are the real goals for which they are striving, what ought to be done in principle in one way or another. . . . Mentally we are living from hand to mouth.

We are slowly beginning to see, however, that in this efficiency-oriented consumer society people need more than ever vacant areas, not occupied by their calling, not completely scheduled for work, where they are freed from the constraints of the industrial mass society; above all, they need leisure periods, to be used intelligently. But it is just this intelligent use of free time which is by no means guaranteed — as we know — by the constantly expanding leisure-time industry: people can be landed in new constraints by an excessive supply of commercial aids to the use of leisure in the longer weekend.

Do we not need to find real repose also within the week-day rhythm, not just externally by sleeping it off or simply doing nothing but also inwardly by true recuperation: to enable us to come to ourselves, to come to our senses, to orient ourselves to our proper goals and norms and thus catch up on ourselves and recuperate?

In this connection does not a well-conducted act of worship provide an irreplaceable opportunity for people (there will be something to be said later about its quality)? It is not God but human beings who gain by our worship. For us it means a great opportunity,

- if in worship we can reactivate our living faith in God and in Christ, a faith that cannot by any means be taken for granted;
- if we thus become once more calm and more composed, get away for a while from the daily pressure and agitation;
- if we are confronted with reliable exemplary values and can again orient ourselves to primary and ultimate standards;
- if we realize that we are bound to a truth;
- if we discover afresh and acquire afresh some meaning in our inconsistent life and in the still more inconsistent history of humankind.

And is it not of the greatest importance for young people to be confronted with exemplary values, standards, and an ultimate horizon of meaning, particularly in a democratic system — an open libertarian-pluralistic system — which of its very nature cannot officially prescribe a *Weltanschauung*, designate in a doctrinaire fashion any supreme values or primary standards, or provide a universal definition of an ultimate meaning? Then they will not lose their bearings, go astray, break down, or despair, still less succumb to a totalitarian system of one color or another with a totalitarian prescription for their orientation.

A good religious service can again provide an ultimate orientation for all the innumerable, inescapable, relevant decisions of life: an orientation which does not abolish freedom but makes it possible in virtue of the commitment to the one true God.

A good *Christian* religious service, however, is a memory of Jesus Christ, continually reactivated by word and meal: a memory of Jesus of Nazareth, made — it is to be hoped — continually freshly alive in his whole visibility and audibility, the basic model to be realized in a variety of ways, inviting people today to a new outlook on life and a new practice of life. Anyone who has experienced this can also testify to the fact that in this way the religious service can really produce for people in their ordinary lives a wider horizon, a clearer line, a firmer conviction and also — to put it quite simply — a little more courage, joy, and freedom for the following week. But now we come to the second consideration.

For the Community's Sake

We do not live our Christian faith in isolation. There is no one who is not dependent on others. That is why the Christian message directs the believer into the community of believers: a community however which should not be self-centered, not an end in itself, but at the service of others. But how is a community to be active in the world, modern society, if it never meets together? For what Jesus wanted should be realized fraternally, in a community.

It is through the religious service that a congregation is formed and continues to be formed afresh as a community of those who are convinced of Christ's cause and prepared to be his disciples: A Church is constituted. For our word "Church" is a translation of *ecclesia*, and *ecclesia* literally means "assembly." A crowd of Christians dispersed throughout the city, if they are more than merely baptized Christians, may amount to something really respectable. But such a mere agglomeration of Christian individuals is not an assembly, a congregation, an *ecclesia*, a Church.

It can be seen that the congregation and its worship are not optional supplements to being a Christian. They are a necessary precondition and at the same time the implementation and concretization of being a Christian: discipleship of Christ implemented and made concrete, to which the individual is in fact challenged but which also needs social realization.

In the concrete, then, what would being a Christian amount to if congregations and their worship were allowed to die? Certainly there can be Christian worship in the ordinary secular routine. But where and how are we to recall the source from which we emerged and from which we must constantly re-emerge if we are to remain Christians? Where are we to recall — thanking, praising, petitioning — the words and deeds, the suffering, dying, and new life of this Jesus of Nazareth, who for Christians must remain the Christ, the authoritative standard? Where, if not in proclamation, in prayer, in meditation, in the hymns and in the meal of the Christian religious service, where at one and the same time we can look back to the source, look forward to a better future, and expect a realistic initiation into the present?

Objections

Should we take part in a religious service only when we feel *what is described as a "need"*? But we may also ask: If we reduce everything to the immediate satisfaction of a need, are we not ruining any sort of friendship, love, marriage, any sort of fellowship, and in fact any community? We have nothing to say against genuine human needs, even in the religious field, although theologians have preached against them far too frequently. Anyone will admit, however, that there are superficial, short-term emotional needs which often arise quite spontaneously. But there are also deeper, more comprehensive needs of human life, of both body and mind, which can be suppressed and of which we must occasionally also be reminded.

It is clear then that prayer and worship are not superfluous luxuries but important and indeed necessary to life, something which must not become stunted if we are to remain fully human, something however which easily declines and even dies if it is not cultivated. These things must not only be talked about but exemplified for children in the life of parents more convincingly than formerly when Christianity and worship were still taken for granted.

Worship is not by any means merely a way of satisfying religious needs, nor is it concerned merely with what is necessary or important for human life. In the last resort — precisely because it is a service of God, a "divine service" — worship involves something more than human beings. It involves God. Quite apart from human needs and aims, apart from whatever is necessary or important, ought it not to be truly appropriate, ought it not to be for us the most utterly human thing also simply and forthrightly to praise and extol our God and Creator, to thank and supplicate God?

Any appeal to the Christian's freedom is irrelevant here. As we saw, when Luther and the Reformers spoke of Christian freedom, they meant something quite different. The Church of Jesus Christ is not a compulsory organization; it is a Church of voluntary members. Their voluntary membership, however, does not exclude but in fact includes obligations and ties voluntarily accepted. Any community which does not insist on a minimum of obligation and participation soon ceases to exist as a community. No community which wants to function internally and externally can be content with merely passive members.

All kinds of clubs and associations have the courage to insist on regular — often weekly — attendance and to some extent closely control this, without their voluntary members feeling that they are subject to compulsion or violence. Should not a church then also have the courage to resist the quest for ease and comfort, however understandable, and expect and demand regular participation as something completely obvious, for the sake of the great common cause, for the sake of God and humankind? Only in this way can we in fact achieve that mutual encouragement in faith on which we are dependent as human beings living among other human beings.

This means for *Catholics:* no legal "Sunday obligation," which has to be fulfilled on pain of "mortal sin." For too long we have instilled fear in people and driven them to church with threats of hell and the devil.

This means for *Protestants:* no more passive acceptance of empty churches in Protestantism. For too long participation in worship (unlike the church tax[1]) has been left completely to the whim of the individual, as a result of a false conception of evangelical freedom. For too long silence has reigned on this obligation, because people lacked the courage of their convictions, when it ought to have been loudly proclaimed; or at most complaints have been aired internally when there ought to have been plain speaking in public.

But however the Protestant churches consider the matter — and they should reconsider it — I would like to hope that in my own church, the Catholic Church, we shall maintain clearly and unmistakably this obvious minimal obligation for the sake of human beings and congregations. We have rightly expressly abolished the precept of Friday abstinence, many obsolete devotions and customs, and long outdated commandments of the Church, or simply dropped them in practice — not least as a service to ecumenism. But regular worship — normally on Sunday or on Saturday evening, if necessary even on a weekday — is neither an antiquated custom nor a secondary matter. While making the most generous allowance for excusing causes in the individual case, any who want to call themselves Catholics should be aware of the fact that in the future also regular participation in the religious service is the minimal obligation expected of them.

---

[1] In Germany all professing Christians are bound by law to make a contribution to their own church (Catholic or Protestant) as part of their income tax. — *Translator.*

A Good Religious Service

Of course any obligation to Sunday worship becomes an insupportable burden whenever the service is carried out in a merely correct way and not well organized. From the time of the Second Vatican Council the Catholic liturgy has taken up and put into effect some of the essential demands of the Reformation. We hear again the Word of God intelligibly proclaimed; all the people take an active part; the liturgy is adapted to different nationalities, simplified, concentrated, and clearly related to Jesus' last supper. Long disputed questions have been settled, at least in principle: Instead of Latin we now have the mother tongue, instead of private Masses a community celebration of the Eucharist, and — at least in certain cases and in smaller groups — communion under both kinds.

In both Catholic and Protestant churches today it depends largely on the individual parish priest or pastor how good, how realistic, how closely related to the situation and how concentrated on the message of Jesus Christ the congregational service in his parish is. And fortunately, despite widespread formalism, ritualistic stereotypes, and excessive intellectualist boredom, we find everywhere today services with life, joy, spontaneity: in brief, services which are really celebrations, truly human festivals, stirred by the Spirit of Jesus Christ. And — this is one of the most gratifying signs of the Church's renewal — the way has been prepared for a new language and a new music which are finding expression in innumerable new prayers and hymns, often quite spontaneously emerging in parochial and student congregations, formulated frequently by young and completely unknown people, or even given shape spontaneously in the course of the service itself.

Unfortunately, not only in Rome but also in the Catholic Church in Germany and elsewhere reactionary trends are becoming stronger. After a successful reform of the Scripture readings, measures are now being introduced, with the aid of a new missal, a uniform hymn book, and superfluous "people's missals" in preconciliar style, to suppress again all spontaneity in worship and to pin down the leaders of our congregations to such "aids" and to very high and hollow-sounding prayers. If we want a service as boring, sterile, and inopportune as possible, if we want to empty our churches still more and to repel young people still more, if we want to breed even more homogeneous and restricted congregations organized according to age, sociological structure, and mentality, even according to clothing and possessions, then we must keep as literally as possible to all these pseudomodern patterns of worship.

Certainly we do not want any irresponsible liturgical adventures or a chaotic liturgy. But neither do we want again a post-Tridentine regimentation, a regulated, high-flown language which leaves the liturgy frozen again for centuries. On the contrary, it must be clearly stated that, however much we want to maintain a firm basic shape and framework, particularly for the eucharistic celebration, not only place and time, ceremonies, vestments, and gestures but also forms of hymns and speech must be treated in principle not as constants but as variables in the service. And the leader of the congregation has not only the right but also the duty (obviously in connection with other congregations and with the whole Church) to look for forms suitable for his congregation and also for good texts. If the official texts and hymns are good, so much the better. But only the best prayers and hymns, wherever they may be found, are good enough for worship today. The criterion must be that they are covered by the Christian message itself and at the same time are completely intelligible for people today. This applies above all — but not only — to us Catholics.

I may be permitted, however, to speak frankly about one problem with which Protestants themselves are very much preoccupied: the neglect of the Lord's Supper in Protestant worship. Certainly being a Christian means the following of Christ in radically human action. Certainly the Word should retain its priority in worship. Certainly the celebration of the meal may not take such a grandiose form as to suggest that carrying out the ritual is the most essential practice of the Church and participation in it the test of a person's Christianity.

But in practice the celebration of the Eucharist in some Protestant churches today presents a very sad spectacle. Or is there any support in the New Testament or in the practice of the early Church for moving the Supper away from the center and making it more an appendage than a constitutive element of Christian worship? Is it permissible for the service of preaching largely to dominate Sundays and the eucharistic service to become an unusual, alien act of worship?

I have no wish to draw up a list of all that is lacking in a service thus reduced to the Word. But, after the Catholic Church in recent years has given expression in its services to so many Protestant concerns and for some of its traditionalists has become more or less "Protestant," there should no longer be any fear on the Protestant side of being accused of "Catholicizing." There should be a resolute commitment to a revaluation of the Supper and thus to a more integrated, truly festal act of worship, making more demands on the individual, stressing the community, appealing more to sight and to imagination than to the intellect.

All this would only be to the advantage of the service of the Word, where the congregation unfortunately is often active only in the singing and in saying the Our Father; it would be understood less intellectually, less subjectively, less individualistically or spiritualistically. For the service of preaching and the service of the meal are not alternatives. They are no more alternatives than are religious services as processes of learning or festive celebrations, with a large congregation or with a small group, with a fixed rite or freely organized.

Prospect

From the very beginning, Sunday for Christians was not merely a postponed Sabbath or a day of rest to be observed in a legalistic spirit but the resurrection day, the Lord's day, on which the Lord's Prayer was said standing and his supper celebrated in the spirit of a family meal.

I would like to invite conservatives and progressives, old and young, Catholics and Protestants to seize once again the opportunity offered for people in our time in the religious service and — it is to be hoped — ever more frequently in a common ecumenical Eucharist. In the Catholic Church in the present century the efforts of many decades were needed to get the congregation actively participating in the liturgy of the Word and particularly in the liturgy of the Eucharist. But it was achieved once the effort had been made to achieve it. Therefore let us renew our striving and now let it be a common effort.

A religious service — properly celebrated — can actually become what we all long for: the feast of our liberation, the precelebration of our final redemption. Seen in this way, a religious service can provide us with a kind of leisure, a genuine free period: the necessary counterweight to working time and the world of achievement, to our ordinary routine; an intimation, a perception, an advance in faith and hope toward a new person, a new creation.

For two thousand years Christians have celebrated their religious service. Is it not to remain so in the future? Is it not to become so again? Rightly understood, the Sunday religious service will never be isolated from the working-day service of God but of itself will lead us into daily life. That is why for the Christian the week begins with Sunday, with Sunday worship as a promise for ordinary daily life and as a signpost to everyday life. *Oratio et actio*, prayer and action, Sunday and working day, attachment to the Church and attachment to the world: these things go together for Christians and their worship, today more than ever.

Part Four —

Betting
on the Future

13

On Fidelity

"He who calls you is faithful, and he will do it."
                                    (1 Thess. 5:25)

Fidelity? Out of curiosity and to amuse myself I recently checked to see what is being said about fidelity in other disciplines. I looked into a dictionary of education, a dictionary of psychology, and a dictionary of sociology: There was no entry for it in any of them. Was Heinrich Heine right when he wrote in his satirical poem "Degeneration" (1844):

> Truth disappears from the earth,
> fidelity's finished too,
> The dogs wag their tails and stink
> as before, but they're no longer true.

Does faithfulness really no longer have any fundamental meaning for practical training, which is what education is really about, for our own psyche, which psychology explores with every possible method, for today's society, which is in so complex a fashion the object of modern sociology?

Fidelity — Essentially "Eternal"

Civil law and the U.N. charter — and common parlance — tell us that certain contracts and duties are to be fulfilled "in good faith," meaning in accordance with their spirit and not just the letter. Unless they are applied with good faith, general principles of law can be perverted into their opposite. This points to something more profound: How can human life together be possible if we can't *trust* one another? To be "true" and to "trust" are kindred actions (both words come from the Indo-European root *deru-* (to be firm or steadfast) , and trust includes all sorts of other things: believing, hoping, waiting (a tryst = a place where one waits trustingly, see the *American Heritage Dictionary*), having confidence in, promising to be true to someone, swearing to keep faith — and, unfortunately, also breaking faith with someone, abusing someone's trust.

Despite the discredit that sometimes attaches in Germany to terms like fidelity and loyalty — with their implications of blind obedience to the Kaiser or the Führer — deep down everybody knows that fidelity, as Schiller says in "Bürgschaft" ("Guarantee") is "yet no empty phantom." It remains fundamental to economic and political life, to the nation and the state, but also to personal comradeship, friendship, love, and marriage. Here we can't do without the trust by which I personally bind myself for the long term beyond the present moment.

Otto Friedrich Bollnow, the prominent Tübingen philosopher and educator, in his early book on *The Nature and Transformation of the Virtues* (1958) stressed that fidelity is a commitment of the person in the present *for the future*. The individual sticks to the obligation incurred in the past *over time* and even *under changed conditions*. Unlike, say, the virtues of perseverance and steadfastness, fidelity is primarily a relationship to concrete others, a relationship that grasps the person in his or her innermost core, and of itself always has an *unconditioned* character. This means that anyone who a priori wants to be true only conditionally will under certain circumstances not be true at all, will be untrue, or faithless. One cannot swear fidelity on condition. True fidelity always means by its very nature "eternal fidelity."

But Still More...

But here our questions naturally set in: We all know how fragile human connections are, how unfathomable are human relationships, how easily in certain situations we let the devil (as we say to excuse ourselves) get hold of us. No, "eternal fidelity" is a phrase we no longer say so readily. For:

How often have friends sworn "to be true forever" in their youth — and soon afterward become estranged.

How often has the phrase "eternal fidelity" been exploited politically and psychologically, too often for people to be allowed to propagate it without some protection.

How often has it been impossible in fact to maintain marital fidelity, although this particularly should be unconditional. For, to echo Bert Brecht, "This old world is not that kind of place" (tr. Eric Bentley).

And so, when another person has broken faith with us, do we then fall into the abyss? Must we despair because we can no longer trust others? Can there possibly be another ground beneath our feet, another dimension in life?

For all the importance of the horizontal dimension, here is where the *vertical dimension* of "eternal fidelity" becomes important. Eternal fidelity — according to the oldest document of the New Testament, the First Letter to the Thessalonians — is the *fidelity of the Eternal himself*. The message of that sentence is not an appeal to eternal fidelity among human beings, as important as that naturally is in the New Testament's perspective.

The message of this sentence is the pledge of fidelity from God: "God is faithful." That God is faithful corresponds, as the Bible sees it, to God's fidelity to himself, a fidelity that finds expression in unswerving constancy and irrevocable steadfastness. God's fidelity is a statement about God's essence that underlines God's trustworthiness in the history of human beings who have so often been unworthy of trust.

But still more than that, when the Psalms speak of God's fidelity, they also continually talk about *God's benevolence, God's grace, God's goodness*, in Hebrew *emet* and *hesed*, in Greek *pistis* and *charis*, in German *Treue* and *Huld*. All this expresses trust that in God we are dealing not with a whimsical superior force, nor with a mysterious Sphinx, nor a two-faced Janus, but with a God of the covenant, a God who stands by what he has bound himself to. We are dealing with a power that is favorably inclined, well disposed to us, which wraps us round and is at work through us, which bears us up and goes before us, which picks us up when we fall. A God who remains true to us even when we are untrue.

If I Don't Listen, God Doesn't Speak

The faithful God, the *theos pistos*: It is remarkable that in the Bible the same Greek word "pistos" means both "faithful" and "believing." And if one reflects, it's easy to see why: Someone who is true is reliable, and someone who is reliable is trustworthy, awakens trust, awakens faith. Conversely, someone who believes in no fidelity can be helped by no fidelity. They are two sides of the same coin.

In other words, *fidelity is bent on faith*. This holds for human beings: between spouses, between friends and partners of every kind. Fidelity is bent on trusting faith. And those who do not continually commit themselves afresh to it will not be helped by any bond or oath of fidelity.

This is true, in the first instance, vis-à-vis *God*, that ineffable, invisible, ungraspable, and yet supremely real power that penetrates our life. If we do not trustfully commit ourselves to God, we will also never perceive

God's fidelity in our lives. If we do not, so to speak, stretch out the wholly personal antenna of our faith, we will not hear the music of the spheres. I cannot discover God's fidelity with X-rays, I cannot empirically ascertain it as a neutral observer. Nothing is "evident" here, and historians will scarcely find anything with historical methods. Nothing will happen here without *reasonable trust:*

> For if I shut myself off, he will not disclose himself;
> if I do not listen, he will not speak;
> if I do not believe, he will not reveal himself.

When he was called, Moses saw the burning bush that was not consumed. And on the long way through the wilderness he wished finally to see God face to face. But he could not. When, according to legend, God in all his glory passed by Moses as he stood in the cleft of the rock, God had to hold his hand over him protectively, lest Moses be blinded by his splendor. Only when God had passed by was Moses allowed to follow him with his eyes: only *from the back* did he see God, not face to face.

The Constant Element in Our Inconstancy

Often we can recognize a pattern in our life only *in retrospect*. Each person has his or her vocation, and the longer our life proceeds, the clearer it will become what our vocation in life is. Non-Christians too have discovered this. *Confucius,* for example, whom I have been studying in recent years, said the following about himself five hundred years before Christ (and on every such birthday one may ask whether one has gotten so far):

> At fifteen I strove for wisdom,
> At thirty I was consolidated within myself.
> At forty there were no more doubts,
> At fifty I knew the *will of heaven.*
> At sixty *my ear was a willing thing*
> To hear in everything only the truth.
> At seventy I could follow the wishes of my heart unreservedly,
> Without overstepping the right measure.

The "will of heaven," the "will of God" is a power that at once points the way and supplies the energy. It is the transcendent dimension immanent in us, which is not only Einstein's fourth dimension, namely, time, at one with the three dimensions of space, but the *dimension of the infinite:* the dimension of *eternity*, which goes beyond every space of time, every space-time.

And in all these years and decades that we pass through so slowly and yet in truth so quickly, this dimension is already *secretly present*, because the Eternal is already present now as the great mystery of our time. The mystery that we come from, the mystery that bears us up, the mystery that waits for us: the unspeakably kind One — constant in our inconstancy, in whose eternal fidelity we may trust beyond death.

This is naturally no cheap generic prescription for getting us through all crises. And what crises haven't we all been through already: vocational problems, sickness, crises in personal relations, in confrontation with institutions. What did I know about the sort of crisis awaiting me when I happily celebrated my fiftieth birthday? And what do I know about the crises that may come after my sixtieth?

In the course of our life histories *we all have the experience of being blocked.* It can happen in major and in minor areas; it can become hard and bitter, and for a long time it can rob you of your sleep. In an undertaking that seems very important not just to me but to others as well, suddenly nothing moves, and my — our — opponents rejoice, "He's been stopped." People — whoever that may be — get in my way, prevent us from moving forward, and that completely changes my situation.

I know only one thing: Things will never again be the way they were, and what will come of it I don't know. I am supposed to come to terms with it, and I cannot, I may not: but the cause should go on. In short I am blocked, with no way out.

...Is God's Concern Alone

What to do then? Resign oneself once and for all, give up, or rebel ...? Take it as one more sign of the absurdity of life? In any case, being stopped is a very tangible challenge, *not only to halt,* but also *to leave off,* to examine myself. It makes no difference whether this is a blockage in my professional life or an unexpected sickness or the breakdown of a personal relationship. Any one of these can be the occasion for reflecting anew on the depth dimension of my life, of opening myself anew in trusting faith.

The experience will be consoling, in that *even in this forced standstill there is something to hold onto,* a stability that is based on the fundamental reality of our life, the first-and-last reality, on the reliable Eternal One himself. God — as the Psalms repeatedly tell us — can provide us with fresh prospects and a way out even in hopeless situations. Drawing upon this trust we will be able to persevere in defeat, to see our lives in a new light, to take a stand again, to correct our course and to take on responsibility anew. Truly, "He who calls you is faithful, and he will do it."

This line recalls to us the basic tension of Christian existence. God's fidelity stands not only at the beginning and in the middle of human life, it also stands at the end. Fidelity lasts *all the way till the completion*. Indeed, fidelity is fidelity only when it goes to the end. "I am sure," says Paul in Phil. 1:6, "that he who began a good work in you will bring it to completion."

God will do it, God will bring it to completion: Completion here does *not* mean *self-completion*, self-perfection, self-justification. As much as we are challenged to achieve, as much as we have to make enormous efforts, professionally and privately, to succeed, to become more mature, better, more perfect, decade after decade, completion does not lie in our hand. The liberating message of this text is: We ourselves need not take care of completion. Completion is God's business alone. We are freed from the pressures and neurotic compulsions to define and realize ourselves by way of our own strivings. We can, by accepting ourselves and our history, arrive at a *peace with ourselves:* based on God's fidelity to us, we can be calmly *faithful to ourselves*.

14

A Vision of a Future Church

Note: This "vision" was drawn up for the meeting of the "Church from below" on the occasion of the pope's second visit to Germany on April 25, 1987, in Cologne, where it was delivered. It contains in its introduction topical material on the current situation that is sufficiently dealt with in this book by Part Two. For this reason I begin immediately with the four crucial future perspectives for the Church.

PERSPECTIVE I: There is a future for a Church connected to its origins and the present, not for a Church infatuated with the past.

The following definitively belong to the past:
1. The model of a *Constantinian-Byzantine imperial Church*, where Church and State harmonized all too well and thought that they themselves had realized the Kingdom of God on earth.
2. And the model of a medieval papal Church, where a theocratically ruling monarch thought he was the absolute master of the Apostolic churches of the East and the churches of the West, indeed of the conscience of all people, and that he could dictate morality even to secular regimes. This was a papally fixated Church, which thinks that even today it can maintain its power with authoritarian regulation, disciplinary sanctions, and political strategies.
3. But also the model of a *Protestant princely or state Church*, where the pope's place is taken by the Prince or the State and the general priesthood of the faithful is dried up into an empty verbal shell.
4. And finally too the model of a financially powerful *modern bureaucratic Church* that has taken refuge in centralization and bureaucratization to defend itself from modern liberalism and socialism: a paradigm of

the Church that is only disguised as modern, but at bottom is a medieval-Counter-Reformation paradigm. This is the pattern that was given sacred legitimization in Vatican I (1870) and again after Vatican II (1962–65), when efforts were made to enforce it with a new old Code of Canon Law, when it was undergirded by a cult of the personality designed to affect the masses and an uncollegial and fully undemocratic personal policy aimed at maintaining Rome's power.

The Church has a future under three conditions:
1. If it reflects on its *origin* and continually reorients itself to the gospel, to Jesus Christ himself.
And this means:

- understanding the Church not as a power structure and a religious multinational corporation, which continually hinders the exercise of dialogue and democracy, but as the people of God and as a community of believers on the scene;
- understanding the Church's office not as a phalanx, or as a "holy rule" (= hierarchy), but as "service" ("diakonia");
- understanding the pope not as a demigod and spiritual autocrat, but as a bishop who leads collegially with his pastoral primacy, bound up with the college of bishops in service to the ecumene.

2. If it preserves the *great Catholic tradition* supported by the gospel (but not the many little Catholic traditions that are by no means always supported by the gospel): continually and decisively oriented to the ancient Christian community, but inspired also by the universal breadth of an Origen and the personal commitment and eloquence of an Augustine, by the ideal of poverty and the nature piety of a Francis of Assisi and the intellectual openness of a Thomas Aquinas, but also by the genuinely evangelical concerns of Luther and Calvin and the Christian life, work, struggles, and sufferings of all our brothers and sisters who lived before us;
3. If finally it looks to the *tasks of the present:*
Then the Church will become a brotherly-sisterly community, joined in solidarity, which does not triumphantly celebrate itself but self-critically admits its enormous shortcomings in Latin America, in China, India, and Africa, and in the First World, openly corrects its mistakes and concentrates on its great task in today's society. And as far as Germany goes: We should have all respect for figures like Rupert Mayer and Edith Stein, who were "beatified" by the pope in Germany for their Christian witness under the Nazis. But we may rightly mistrust this sort

of medieval church custom, when the brave resistance of individuals amid general conformism by the Church is used for papal promotion, for the repression and rejection of guilt, instead of for clear confession of responsibility.

Are these all just hopeless illusions? In no way: *The Church's new future has already begun!* For we can attest that the new future begins *from below*. It has dawned:

- wherever a *pastor* (there are more than people think) does not simply parrot the notions of his Roman-German Church superiors (on issues such as birth control, mixed marriage, admission of divorced persons to the sacraments, exercise of authority, admitting the Church's errors, the Third World, and liberation theology), but thinks, feels, and acts with the men and women of his community;

- wherever a *bishop* (an Oscar Romero, Helder Camara, Evaristo Arns, Aloisio Lorscheider, Raymond Hunthausen), when confrontations occur, does not simply follow the line of the Vatican, but — as a "good shepherd," not a "hireling" — in the spirit of Jesus identifies primarily with the men and women of his diocese and his region;

- wherever a *pope* (as a John XXIV may perhaps again show) orients himself, not to the pressures of the Roman system, but to the demands of the gospel and the needs of today's men and women, and thus champions the *aggiornamento* of the Church, the ecumene, full catholicity and critical evangelical commitment in words and deeds. Then indeed he belongs to the Church from below, then he relates not as the supreme master, teacher, and judge of God's Church. Then he is what he is supposed to be, according to the phrase of Gregory the Great, a successor of the modest and sympathetic, fallible Galilean fisherman, Peter, the "servant of the servants of God."

PERSPECTIVE II: There is a future not for a Church of patriarchy, but for a Church of partnership.

The time has passed:

1. For *stereotyped images of women:* Women no longer accept in silence what Church functionaries and theologians have to say about them, "their" nature and "their" — obviously unique — role in the Church and society. They resist having to live up to images fashioned by men. As grown-up Christians they themselves want and are able to determine who they are — each in her own way — and where each one sees her task.

2. For *one-track language:* Women no longer put up with an ecclesi-

astical, liturgical, and theological language that excludes them, makes them invisible, passes over them in silence. They are unwilling to be "included" by the Church as "brothers" and "sons." They are no longer prepared to speak about and to God in terms taken exclusively from the experience of men. Increasingly women claim the right to name for themselves what God means for them and for their lives. They will no longer let the domination of men and the oppression of women go unchallenged in the name of God the Father and Jesus the man.

3. For *pre-established gender roles:* Women no longer accept being "silent and in all subjection," as Church practice has de facto dealt with them: from the ban on women acolytes to the ban on the ordination of women and "artificial" birth control there has been a single strand of regimentation. Women will no longer allow themselves to be degraded into the objects of masculine commandments, prohibitions, rules, and role directives. Every form of domination and authority that attempts to impose its will upon others instead of promoting them in their process of personal evolution will be judged by women not just as untimely and unjust, but as a sin. Women are increasingly resisting such pressures and at the same time working for a different kind of Church.

The Church has a future only under three further conditions:

1. If *everyone is converted:* If all of us, women and men, no longer tolerate sexism and patriarchalism. So long as power in the Church rests only in the hands of men, while women are expected to serve out of love and to represent the caring, humanitarian element, the fundamental Christian unity of power, justice, and love will be torn asunder and corrupted.

2. If we, *all of us,* act: if in a sexist, patriarchal world we succeed in bearing credible witness to God as the God of liberation and redemption and God's goodness in word and deed: We may not just give lip service to everyone's being equal in the sight of God. We must, particularly in the Church, actively resist the division of people into first- and second-class citizens.

3. If clericalism comes to a halt and *office and charism in the Church again form an unrenounceable unity:* The most important criteria for an office in the Church may no longer be masculine gender and an opportunistic, conformist affirmation of the status quo. Rather we should be serious about there being different capacities, vocations, and charisms that contribute to the building up of a partnership-community of women and men in the Church.

Is this all an empty demand? By no means: *The future of a Church oriented to partnership has already begun.* For that is what we demonstrate, men and women, together: the Church of partnership grows *from below:*

- All over the world women have begun to discover sexism and patriarchalism in the Christian Church and theology. They no longer simply accept the ecclesiastical and theological structures of the subordination of women, but criticize them publicly as an expression of unjust and unjustified domination.

- For many women the phase of simply raising questions is obviously past, along with the time of waiting for the official Church to respond to their requests and demands. Women are taking the liberty of acting in accordance with their own understanding of Christian faith — in the awareness that they themselves are the Church too.

- Being Christian means for them starting out from the idea that "in Christ there is neither male nor female" (Gal. 3:28), the duty of standing up for liberation from oppression into a life of human dignity and self-determination for everyone here and now.

PERSPECTIVE III: There is a future not for a narrow denominational Church, but for an ecumenically open one.

The time has passed:

1. For *denominational exclusivity:* Since the documents of Vatican II, at the vary latest, it is no longer permissible for a single denomination to pass itself off as the one, holy, uniquely true Church of Jesus Christ, outside of which no one can come to salvation. In this spirit countless Christians can no longer accept churches' excluding one another because of contradictory teachings, raising their barriers even within families, and Christians' discriminating against one another because of their conflicting denominational affiliations.

2. For *denominational usurpation of office:* Thousands of Catholics, laypeople and ordained priests, no longer accept the idea that the official acts of Protestant ministers (above all in the Eucharist) are looked upon as invalid, that entering upon a mixed marriage is considered an offense against faith, that active participation in Protestant worship rates as a religious crime, that ecumenical services are strictly forbidden on Sunday.

3. For *denominational refusal of fellowship:* In all churches the majority of believers no longer understands why one church should exclude another from eucharistic fellowship and look upon the sacraments (except for, at best, baptism) as ineffectual or superfluous. This denial of fellowship is contrary to the spirit of Jesus, who invited everyone, and

especially those excluded from pious society, to his table. Such denial is also contrary to the spirit of the early Christian community, which looked upon eucharistic fellowship as a sign of the unity despite all differences of status, education, gender, and theology.

The Church has a future but only under three conditions:

1. That it *practices on the inside* what it preaches on the outside: What good is it if the Church's hierarchs demand reconciliation, peace, justice, and freedom from the world, while they themselves hinder the reconciliation of communities, while they delay the coming of peace to the Christian world, while they trample on justice in the Church — vis-à-vis theologians, nuns, women in general — and suppress the freedom of episcopal elections and theological research? What good is it if on his trip to the Ruhr the pope speaks out against unemployment in society but fails to do everything he can to lessen unemployment in the Church, e.g., by giving work to jobless lay theologians, who are badly needed by our increasingly priestless parishes?

2. That it finally follows up the countless ecumenical words, gestures, and prayers with *ecumenical deeds:* How should it be credible when despite the largely successful approximation of standpoints in dialogue between the churches the official Church insists on the remaining differences? It is high time for the Church's leadership seriously to translate into action the results of its own ecumenical dialogue commission. One first step would be for the pope, while on this sort of visit to Germany, not to hold another liturgy of the Word with no binding practical consequences, but to issue a solemn declaration lifting the excommunication of Martin Luther and the anathemas dating from the Reformation period.

3. That it *continues the renewal* initiated by Vatican II. It is counterproductive for the Church both worldwide and locally, when the pope and bishops begin once again to throttle rather than promote the ecumenical fellowship that in many communities has grown for years; when those who otherwise overwhelm pastors and parishes with paperwork scarcely anyone reads, do not finally introduce concrete steps toward unity through realistic plans for union.

But is all this perhaps just ecumenical wish fulfillment? Far from it, *the ecumenical future of the Church has already begun.* For, as many people will attest, the ecumenically open Church grows from below:

- For years countless Protestant and Catholic theologians all over the world have been unobtrusively teaching and doing research, unafraid of intrusions on their careers, working on the sensitive issues that

160

divide the churches. Through this work they have made it possible to cancel the division between the churches.

- A complex practical cooperation between religious communities has developed on location in the realms of education and social life, in youth work, counselling, and care for the elderly, in cooperation for peace and development.

- In our schools many young people as a matter of course select their own religion teacher. Families from mixed marriages have often long respected the practice of the other church and actively taken part in it.

- Indeed, countless providers of pastoral care in the divided churches have mutually recognized one another. They have taken joint responsibility for the preaching of the gospel, not least of all because they have realized that the dividing line nowadays runs increasingly between belief and unbelief rather than between the denominations.

- In many communities throughout the world, eucharistic hospitality has long been practiced without creating any stir and understood as an expression of already achieved religious communion.

PERSPECTIVE IV: There is a future not for a Eurocentric but for a universal Church.

The time has passed:

1. For *absolutist Christian claims:* Since Vatican II the self-righteous conviction that Christian faith is the only legitimate religion has lost ground, in the churches of the World Council as well. No longer are Christians so certain that their faith alone has a claim on everyone's respect without having to pay such respect to others too. The fact that other religions are being defamed as a diabolical product of human ignorance, self-justification, and arrogance is increasingly seen as incompatible with the spirit of the Nazarene, who brought sympathy, indeed love, to bear on so many non-Jews.

2. For *European colonialism:* In the period that Europeans call modernity, religious and economic expansion, undergirded by military interests, wantonly and deliberately destroyed other religions and cultures — in the name of Christ — above all in Latin America and Africa. Nowadays this is bemoaned by many Christians, but seldom admitted as the Church's fault by many of the Church's princes. Kissing the ground upon arriving in foreign countries is one thing, and fine as far as it goes. But a clear confession of the Church's monstrous history of guilt and

of its shared responsibility for the wretched social conditions in these countries is another thing, and better.

Many Christians, from South Africa to Chile, are awaiting from the Church a clear and unambiguous statement about resistance to exploitative dictators and repressive political structures. Our Church is still too much involved with the dominating interests of the First World. Wherever the Church makes the people's interests its own (e.g. Haiti, the Philippines), democratic achievements are possible (one hopes this will soon be the case in Chile and South Africa too).

3. For *Roman imperialism:* Open-minded Europeans of all denominations will no longer tolerate both old, established churches and young ones on other continents being kept in leading strings. They reject the Roman imperialism that seeks to bind all churches to an outdated medieval system of law and piety. The three demands by the Chinese for self-support, self-government, and self-propagation of the regional and national churches correspond not only to the contemporary understanding of democracy. They also thoroughly correspond to the early Christian constitution of the Church and the great Catholic tradition of the first millennium.

But the Church has a future only under three premises:

1. Insofar as it has *respect for the ever greater truth.* For with all its claim to the truth the Church has no monopoly on it. It must face the challenge of the claim to truth made by other religions without fearing to lose its identity.

2. Insofar as it also seeks to *learn from the other religions:* In respecting the other religions the Church is challenged to take up the often repressed riches of the other religions so as to deepen its own practice: all the aesthetic, meditative, and liturgical traditions of the others — with syncretistic combinations.

3. Insofar as it leaves the various *national, regional, and local churches an appropriate autonomy:* churches have to be able to shape their style of life and organization on their own responsibility, altogether in keeping with the richness and God-given variety of human history.

Nevertheless isn't all this purely utopian? Not at all, this *global future of the Church has already begun.* For, as we know, the Church grows *from below:*

- From East Africa to Latin America, from India to Burma, Thailand, and Korea base groups and "small Christian communities" for self-help and love of neighbor are taking concrete shape beyond all the limits of religion and ideology.

162

- In the churches of Africa in particular people are opening up more to the artistic traditions, the dances, and spontaneous joy in life of Africans. At the same time they are trying to resist foreign control by westernization brought by the forces ruling Africa.

- In many meditation centers and religious communities of America, Europe, and Germany, as in the ashrams of India, we find silence practiced rather than dogmatic disputatiousness, community exchanges with people having different opinions rather than hierarchical indoctrination, spontaneous readiness for participation in the life of others rather than stiff distance — and all this combining greater spiritual-mystical intensity with sociopolitical commitment.

What then do we hope for?

We do not know how these four perspectives of a future Church will be realized in concrete particulars. No one of us is so naive as to believe that the Catholic Church will automatically grow again through structural reforms alone (the Protestant churches, whose problems obviously lie elsewhere, prove the opposite). But without such changes the future will be lost, and the conflict must increase between an all too stubborn, security-conscious, dominating Upper Church and the innovative pressures from activist groups oriented to problems and conflicts.

No, we don't know how the Church of the third millennium after Christ will look. But despite all moroseness, all skepticism, all widespread cynicism, we will not give up the hope that the Church, which has already begun to grow from below, will finally, as in the conciliar period, burst upward and blossom. On what basis? "No other foundation can any one lay than that which is laid, which is Jesus Christ" (1 Cor. 3:11). By what standard? "I am," said Jesus (John 14:6), "the way, and the truth, and the life." Given the standard of the message and the fate of Jesus of Nazareth, his death, and his awakening to eternal life, a double law holds for us: The often so misanthropic and bureaucratic Church must die and the philanthropic Church of Jesus must again and again resurrect in our hearts.

The Church with a misanthropic-bureaucratic face must *die*. A Church must die,

- in which the *evil spirit* of dogmatic immobility, moralistic censorship, and legalistic insurance and sanctions has become dominant;

- in which *fear* of the downfall of what has been coddled for centuries dominates and is ascribed to the influence of the devil;

163

- in which the *Philistine mentality* of bureaucrats in professorial chairs predominates. This is the mentality of moralistic dogmatizers on church commissions, of official spokesmen in church-dominated media. Vatican financial scandals involving billions of dollars, unexplained ties to the Mafia, and mysterious accidental deaths would disappear once and for all, and a transparent financial policy would take its place. And the so-called Opus Dei — a financially powerful secret league in the spirit of the Spanish Counter-Reformation with fascist-style features — would no longer be encouraged from the very top, enabling it to throw its weight around in our Church with impunity, long after secret societies like the Freemasons have been condemned and excommunicated.

But conversely too the *philanthropic Church of Jesus* must continually *resurrect* in our hearts. For in the spirit of Jesus, the spirit of solidarity with all humanity, we can:

- dispense with *discrimination and the Inquisition among us:* People like Leonardo Boff in Brazil, Edward Schillebeeckx in Holland, Jacques Pohier in France, Charles Curran in the United States, George Bulanyi in Hungary, and countless other unknown theologians in Asia and Africa would have nothing more to fear. At a time when even the Kremlin is beginning to rehabilitate its dissidents, we will truly be able to question what the Vatican intends to do with its own. Does it mean to go on in the spirit of the Inquisition which has led many of us to resignation and some even to the edge of psycho-physical exhaustion and professional destruction?

- *exercise forgiveness and dare a new beginning* instead of reckoning up the historical guilt of the different churches and religions: Intercommunion would no longer be a fighting word, and the welcome religious gathering in Assisi with representatives of other religions would be no mayfly phenomenon.

- *make a new social and political commitment:*
    — in the peace movement, not just for disarmament, but more profoundly against the arms madness, for a spirit of peaceableness on all levels (including private life);
    — in the ecology movement, not just for humane modes of production and consumption, but more profoundly against the madness of spending, for a spirit of rebirth, of a new basic attitude, a new scale of values in our lives (including our private lives);

— in the social movement, not only for more social obligations, but more profoundly against the madness of competition, for a different spirit of worldwide economic partnership and distribution.

This then is the foundation of our *docta spes*, our "tested hope": Where the Spirit rules, the Church already has a future. For this reason we can keep our hopes alive.

Part Five —

Epilogue

15 —

My Personal *Spero* —
The Vision of a Better Future

When a man has sixty years behind him his curiosity increases as he asks himself which of his expectations may still be fulfilled. And he is likewise more serious than before in his concern that the things for which he studied and battled, worked and suffered, outlive him. That is why I gladly use the opportunity offered me by this "testament" to speak of my vision of a better future, a vision which still sustains me today and can perhaps sustain others as well. Despite everything, despite the possibility of human self-destruction, whether slow or sudden, my personal *spero*, my personal hope, which is of course based in my *credo*, in my faith of Jewish-Christian origin, persists. It is a *spero* which has constantly expanded for me in the course of the decades: from churches to religions and eventually to nations.

Ad primum: A whole theological life long I have been committed to the renewal of the Catholic Church and its theology and to an ecumenical understanding between the Christian churches. I have been able to see progress, especially under Pope John XXIII and during the Second Vatican Council. Much that had for centuries been considered impossible within the Catholic sphere was realized "overnight": a heightened appreciation of the Bible and its proclamation, of charisms and the laity, the vernacular in the liturgy and the chalice for the laity, an easing in questions of mixed marriages and religious instruction, the collaboration of Christian churches in many areas of society and culture, the formation of ecumenical commissions to iron out the questions which still separate the churches....

But I have also had to accept setbacks, especially under the popes of the 1970s and 1980s. The ecumenical euphoria petered out, initiatives bogged down, committed consensus documents disappeared into Vatican drawers. Instead of *aggiornamento*, Restoration. Instead of ecumenical accomplishments, ecumenical phrases and unecumenical obstructions. Instead of collegiality, once again the old authoritarianism, and instead of dialogue, only too often the arrogance of power and the suppression of other views. Equal rights, especially for women, are denied now as before; once again theologians are increasingly excluded or removed from professorial chairs controlled by the Church; only representatives loyal to the Roman line are named bishops. An atmosphere of stagnation and resignation is spreading. From the beginning I was aware of how intensely those in power in Rome — and not seldom in other Christian churches as well — would resist any modification of church structure to fit the standard of the gospel itself and the demands of the time.

Yet *spero contra spem*, I hope against all hope! Despite everything I do not give up hope. An *oikoumenē* among the Christian confessions is possible, indeed necessary! The dogmas of human origin separating the churches will fade before God's truth; the medieval-premodern structures which treat people, women especially, as underprivileged will disintegrate; the overbearing ecclesiastical authorities who have arrogated rights to themselves over the centuries will be cut down to human scale:

- Someday all the medieval and early-modern privileges and pretensions of the *Catholic* Church vis-à-vis the other Christian churches, their offices and worship, will have been outgrown; infallibilist papalism and pseudo-Christian papal idolatry will have disappeared in favor of a Petrine office at the service of all Christianity, within the framework of synodal and conciliar structures. A John XXIV will come forth in the model of Pope John XXIII.

- But the regional provincialism and biblicistic fundamentalism of *Protestant* provenance will also give way to a Church responsible to the world and to that enlightened "freedom of the Christian" which exhibits neither moralizing self-righteousness nor dogmatic intolerance.

- And an *Orthodox* traditionalism and ritualism will be transcended, changed in favor of a Christianity simultaneously closer to its origins and more contemporary. Not the least of the results will be a worship which can exercise a leavening function in the transformation of politics and society in the countries of Eastern Europe.

That is my hope. No, not a uniform single Church; the confessional, regional, even national character of the Christian churches will not be melted down. Rather an ecumenical unity among the Christian churches: reconciled in diversity. An idiotically extravagant hope? No, a realistic vision, one whose realization has already begun at the grassroots of the churches.

Ad secundum: As a Christian theologian I have increasingly advocated changing the attitude of Christian churches toward the non-Christian religions of the world. I have been able to see progress — in the decrees of the Second Vatican Council on freedom of conscience and religion, in the declarations on Judaism, Islam, and the other world religions. And then after the Council all the many encounters between people of different religions; all the common efforts for peace and human rights across all religious boundaries; all the increased study of one another's traditions by theologians, religious scholars, philosophers throughout the world; all the effort toward genuine encounter in meditation and action, in authentic dialogue.

But here too there were setbacks: wars on our globe still continue to be supported or legitimated by religions; there is still prejudice and rejection, indeed enmity and hate between believers of various religions; many Christians still self-righteously believe in the unconditional superiority and the absolute claims of their own religion; ecumenical understanding is still suspect as syncretism, relativism, and diffusiveness. From the beginning I was aware that in all religions there are power structures which have no interest in ecumenical openness, in reciprocal information and human transformation, structures whose efforts are directed rather to drawing boundaries, to apologetics, to disparaging others.

Yet *spero contra spem*, I hope against all hope! Despite everything I do not give up hope: an *oikoumenē* among the religions of this earth is possible, is necessary, for there can be no peace among nations without peace among religions. But there will be no peace among religions without dialogue among religions:

- More and more people will realize that the three great prophetic religions — Judaism, Christianity, and Islam — form one connected religious river-system springing out of the Semitic Near East, with members who also profess belief in the one God of Abraham as the Creator and Sustainer of this world, in a course of history pointing to the future, in a fundamentally moral ethos of elementary humanity (the Ten Commandments).

- More and more, in the ecumenical spirit of reconciliation, we will learn that we must also let ourselves be enriched by a second great

171

river-system, which originates in Indian mysticism (Hinduism and Buddhism especially), and by a third, which flows from Chinese wisdom (Confucianism, Taoism): by their spiritual values, by their mystical depth, by their views of world and humanity tested over the centuries.

- More and more the three great prophetic religions themselves will share their own limitless intellectual-spiritual heritage with others moving far beyond any religious colonization, far beyond any triumphalistic grandeur, far beyond any intellectual disparagement or assimilation.

That is my hope. No, not a unity of religions, not a single religion, a religious stew or syncretic mishmash. But an ecumenical peace among world religions! And that means a peaceful coexistence, a growing convergence, and a creative proexistence of religions in the common search for the always greater truth and the mystery of the one and true God which will be fully revealed only in the eschaton. An empty utopia? No, a realistic vision, whose realization has already begun at the religious grassroots.

Ad tertium: From a good three decades of experience in international theology I have come to know the Church as a global community of faith, integrating all nations and races. Increasingly I have confronted the theological task from a global, international perspective. From numerous travels around the world and countless hours of quiet study day and night I have learned that theology must contribute its share to an understanding among nations. The consequences of such an understanding are visible: centuries-old "hereditary enemies" like Germany and France have overcome their hatreds; the process of forming a community of countries in Western Europe moves along despite all bottlenecks and barriers; the recent relaxing of tensions between East and West is obvious; and the development of trust and conversations on disarmament are finally leading to concrete results; the development of international understanding, of economic and cultural cooperation appears necessary for survival and therefore irreversible. . . .

But setbacks have occurred as well: alongside the process of integration in Europe and the beginning of an understanding between East and West stands a process of growing division between North and South. The disparities between the rich and poor nations grow unceasingly: the people of this earth are more than ever divided socially and ecologically — as well as economically by the debt crisis. The exploitation of air, water, and earth with harmful substances and trash has reached shocking dimensions. From the beginning I was aware that there are power cartels in this world with an interest in the continuation of such exploitative processes, especially in the Third and Fourth Worlds — cartels which seek to hinder the creation of a just world economic order.

Yet *spero contra spem*, I hope against all hope! Despite everything I do not give up hope: an *oikoumenē* among nations is possible, is necessary. And then, in a comprehensive ecumenical fashion, the religions of the world — in North and South, West and East — will be able to realize in a quite new way their moral responsibility

- for peace and thus an end to international hostilities;
- for justice and thus the elimination of unjust social and political structures;
- for the preservation of creation and thus the maintenance of an inhabitable and hospitable earth.

That is my hope: No, not an all-powerful world regime or world bureaucracy; no domination in the name of religion; no old or new physical or spiritual coercion on behalf of religious juridicism, dogmatism, or moralism; no authoritarian exercise of power by hierarchs or bonzes, ayatollahs or gurus. On the contrary! Freedom for and even solidarity with both believers and the many doubters hesitating between faith and disbelief! An ecumenical community among the peoples, a true "united nations": and in their service a religion and spirituality whose deepest human basic intentions — the salvation of the entire person and all persons — will be recognized and realized by the people themselves. All a desperate mirage? No, a realistic vision, whose realization has already begun at the grassroots of the nations.

In summa:

  Spero unitatem ecclesiarum: I hope for the unity of the churches.
  Spero pacem religionum: I hope for peace among religions.
  Spero communitatem nationum: I hope for community among nations.
  Where does the strength of my hope come from? For me personally, as for millions of religious people throughout the world, the basis of my hope is that utterly reasonable trust which is called faith:

  "In Te, Domine, Speravi; non confundar in aeternum."
"In Thee, O Lord, have I hoped; I shall not be confounded in eternity."

Part Six —

Documentation

16

Declaration
"For the Freedom of Theology"
(1968)

In full loyalty and unequivocal fidelity to the Catholic Church we, the undersigned theologians, consider ourselves prompted and obliged to make the following point publicly and with great seriousness: The freedom won for theologians and theology by the Second Vatican Council for service to the Church must not be placed at risk again today. This freedom is a fruit of, and a challenge from, the liberating message of Jesus himself and remains an essential aspect of the freedom of God's children in the Church as proclaimed and defended by Paul. For this reason it is incumbent on all teachers in the Church to preach the Word in season and out of season, whether convenient or not.

For us theologians this freedom implies at the same time a grave responsibility not to imperil the genuine unity and the true peace of the Church. We are well aware that we theologians too can be mistaken in our theology. But we are convinced that erroneous theological notions cannot be gotten rid of by compulsory measures. In our world they can be effectively corrected only through unimpeded, objective, scholarly discussion, where truth can triumph on its own. We affirm with conviction the magisterium of the pope and the bishops, subject to the Word of God and in the service of the Church and its preaching. But we also know that this pastoral preaching office must not repress or hinder the theologians' scholarly task of teaching. Every kind of Inquisition, however subtle, does not just harm the development of healthy theology. It also does incalculable damage to the credibility of the entire Church in today's world. That is why we expect that the pope and the bishops in their preaching office will take for granted our thinking with the Church and support without prejudice our theological work for the welfare of the men and women in the Church and the world. We would like to comply with our duty of seeking and speaking the truth without hindrance from administrative measures and sanctions. We expect our freedom to be respected whenever we speak out or publish our well- founded theological convictions, to the best of our knowledge and belief.

Since the threat to free theological work now seems to be on the increase again, we feel obliged to make a series of constructive proposals. We consider their implementation indispensable, so that the pope and bishops can appropriately and worthily meet their responsibilities, which also extend to the function of theologians in the Church.

1. The authorities of the Roman curia, especially the Congregation for the Doctrine of the Faith, have been to a certain degree internationalized by Pope Paul VI. But they will be exposed to the appearance of partisan bias, for the sake of a certain theological party line, so long as they do not clearly take into account the legitimate multiplicity of today's theological schools and mentalities in the make-up of their personnel.

2. This applies in the first instance to the decision-making organ of the Congregation for the Doctrine of the Faith, the plenary assembly of cardinals (*Plenaria*). Here the age limit of seventy-five should be introduced.

3. Only proven and generally recognized experts should be appointed as consultants. Their time in office has to be specifically limited and should under no circumstances exceed the age of seventy-five.

4. The international commission of theologians called for by the Episcopal Synod should be set up immediately. It should embrace the various theological orientations and mentalities in the Church. The Congregation for the Doctrine of the Faith should cooperate as closely as possible. Also the jurisdiction of the Congregation and the episcopal commissions within the Bishops Conference dealing with questions of faith should be clearly and fundamentally delineated.

5. In extraordinary and weighty individual cases the Congregation for the Doctrine of the Faith may feel obliged to raise objections against a theologian or group of theologians. In each such situation (not excepting individuals in religious orders) an orderly procedure has to be followed. In keeping with the directives of the pope for the reform of the Holy Office ("Integrae Servandae," of December 7, 1965), a clear and binding procedure has to be worked out and at last properly published. The jurisdiction of the Congregation for the Doctrine of the Faith should be clearly limited to theological issues. On purely personal matters only the orderly path of law can be taken.

6. In the procedural regulations, which should also be reflected in the revised Code of Canon Law, the following must be guaranteed;

a. The scrutiny of matters of faith by the Congregation has to be carried out on the basis of authentic publications by the author himself in the original language, not on the basis of unauthorized reports or translations. From the outset the Congregation should appoint an official defender of the theologian in question (*relator pro auctore*). After the examination has taken place all the objectionable teachings are to be communicated to the theologian in question with whatever reports, decrees, *relationes*, and important documents may be under consideration. The theologian will present his position on this material in writing.

b. If that position is found to be unsatisfactory, two or more expert reports on the disputed questions by recognized theologians are to be brought in. At least one half of the experts can be designated by the theologian himself.

c. After this, if personal discussions are thought to be necessary, the names of the interlocutors, the subject of the conversation, and the complete text of all relevant reports, decrees, and other important minutes and documents should be shared with the theologian in question well beforehand. The theologian can carry on the conversation in any language he wishes and may bring with him an expert consultant for support. There is no obligation to keep the transactions secret. Minutes of the conversation will be drawn up, signed by all the participants, and sent to the Congregation.

d. If even after this colloquium the Congregation judges that there is unequivocal proof that the doctrines under attack unequivocally contradict the truly binding confession of the Church and endanger a wide range of believers, the Congregation shall publicly refute these teachings in a well-grounded position paper.

e. Without prejudice to the binding nature of the Church's doctrinal authority, in today's society any further administrative or financial measures against authors or publishing houses should as a rule be omitted as useless or even harmful.

7. Since all faith without love is nothing, in all efforts to seek truth in the Church the principles of Christian charity must be followed.

Postscript

This declaration, sketched out by the author and edited by the theologians Yves Congar, Karl Rahner, and Edward Schillebeeckx, was published by the Executive Committee of *Concilium*, the international theological journal. It was ultimately signed by 1360 Catholic theologians, men and women, from all over the world. The Congregation for the Doctrine of the Faith thereupon issued a procedural ordinance that accepts some of the desiderata put forth; but it ignored, and to this day still ignores, the most important ones.

17

Declaration "Against Resignation" (1972)

The Catholic Church finds itself in a multi-leveled crisis of leadership and trust. Six years after the Second Vatican Council the third Roman Episcopal Synod has come to an end without palpable results. In the conciliar period the Church's leadership tackled both old and new questions and to an astonishing extent led the way toward solutions. But now in the postconciliar period it seems incapable of achieving constructive results on such urgent issues as peace and justice in the world and the crisis of the Church's office. The essentially peripheral law of celibacy has undeservedly become a test question for church renewal. But while the official church authorities facing very different sorts of difficulties content themselves with complaints and admonitions or else have recourse to arbitrary sanctions, more and more priests are giving up their duties, and the next generation is declining in both quantity and quality.

The perplexity of many members of the Church is great, and many of the best pastors have the impression that in their crucial concerns they have been left in the lurch by their bishops and often by the theologians too. It is true that some episcopal offices and a few bishops have in all seriousness made the concerns of their churches their own. But most of the bishops' conferences have been able to reach constructive solutions only on less important questions, and have disappointed many expectations of the clergy and people. Thus the credibility of the Catholic Church, which at the beginning of the pontificate of Paul VI may have been higher than at any other time in the last five hundred years, has sunk to a disturbing degree. Many people are suffering because of the Church. Resignation is spreading.

If we look for reasons — and this can be done only in summary fashion — for the current crisis in leadership and trust, we may not look for them simply in certain persons, and certainly not in their ill will. The cause is rather the Church's system itself, which has remained far behind the times in its development and still displays numerous features of princely absolutism: popes and bishops as de facto largely autocratic lords of the Church, uniting legislative, executive, and judicial functions in their hands. Despite the councils that have meantime been established, their exercise of power is in many places subject to no real control, and their successors are chosen according to criteria of conformity. There are widespread complaints in various parts of the Church about the appointment of bishops by secret procedures, about the lack of openness in the decision process, about the hierarchy's continual invoking its own authority and the obedience of the others, about insufficient motivation for claims and directives, about a monocratic style of office that disregards genuine collegiality, about keeping in tutelage the laity and the "lower clergy," who can raise no effective objection to the decisions of the authorities. They demand freedom for the Church in the outside world but inside they do not grant it. Peace and justice are preached where it costs the Church and its leaders nothing. Secondary issues are fought over, thereby ignoring both major concepts affecting the future and clear present priorities. Even hesitant attempts by theology to help the Church in this situation are met with mistrust and resistance. This leads to passivity on the part of many members of the Church and growing apathy to the Church's spokesmen among the general public.

Today the issue is not just the so-called democratization of the Church. If we get to the bottom of the current lack of leadership and theory in the Church, we keep finding that the Church has remained not only far behind the times, but also, and above all, behind its own mandate. As both friends and foes have judged, it has not followed in the footsteps of the man it continually invokes. That is why we can see a peculiar contrast between the interest in Jesus himself and the disinterest in the Church. Wherever the Church exercises its power over humanity instead of serving it, wherever the Church's institutions, teachings, and laws become an end in themselves, wherever its spokesmen present their personal opinions and agenda as divine commandments and dispositions, then the Church's mandate is betrayed, the Church distances itself at once from God and human beings, it falls into crisis.

This crisis can be overcome only if the whole Church — pope, bishops, pastors, religious, theologians, and lay people again consider their *center and foundation: the gospel of Jesus Christ*, from which it took its start and which it has to understand and live anew in every new situation. What this means in the various countries, cultures, and areas of life, what it means, in principle and concretely, for the individual and the community, cannot be developed here. No detailed program of reform will be sketched out here. There is no lack of programs; the ones we have are just not carried out. But the one question that is so distressing and depressing these days *can* be answered: Does such an appeal still make sense? Don't the superior force and the closed nature of the Church's system block any serious reform? In this difficult hour that the Church now faces is there any path between revolution and resignation? Still, the question can also be put the other way around: Might not the situation in the Catholic Church be suddenly transformed, if the current credibility gap, the crisis in leadership and trust, were overcome? Just waiting for a change at the top would certainly be foolish.

As theologians we have no intention of laying presumptuous claim to the leadership functions. But neither can we withdraw from our shared responsibility for our Church. We wish to make our own the concerns of many people within and without the Catholic Church, as we try, aware of our responsibility, to lay down a few helpful (we hope) points of orientation aimed at overcoming stagnation and resignation. How should we behave in this situation?

No Silence
The demands of the gospel and the troubles and hopes of our time are, on many of the issues facing us, so clear that silence out of opportunism, cowardice, or superficiality can be as wrong as the silence of many responsible persons during the Reformation period.

And So:
Those bishops — within the national bishops conferences they often make up a strong minority or even the majority — who consider certain laws, ordinances, and measures a disaster, should come out and say this publicly and call straightforwardly for change. The size of the majority in all decisions of the bishops conferences may no longer be withheld from public scrutiny in the Church today. But theologians too can no longer appeal to scholarship as a way of keeping out of the questions concerning life in the Church. They have to take an appropriate stand wherever crucial matters affecting the Church and the findings in their field of expertise are at stake. Everyone in the Church, whether an office-holder or not, whether man or woman, has the right and often the duty to say whatever he or she thinks about the Church and its leadership and whatever he or she believes it is necessary to do. Of course, one should take a stand just as clearly against tendencies toward disintegration as against tendencies toward petrifaction.

Personal Action

Too many people in the Catholic Church make accusations and complaints about Rome and the bishops without doing anything themselves. If the parish liturgy is boring nowadays, if pastoral care is ineffective, theology sterile, openness to the needs of the world limited, and ecumenical cooperation with the other Christian communities minimal, the responsibility for this cannot be simply shoved off onto the pope and the episcopacy.

And So:

Whether one is a pastor, chaplain, or layperson, all members of the Church have to do something themselves to help the renewal of the Church in their domain of life, large or small. And in modern society particularly the individual has possibilities of positively influencing the Church's life. In various ways one can press for better forms of worship, more intelligible preaching, and more relevant pastoral care, for ecumenical integration of communities and Christian commitment in society.

Acting Together

One parishioner who goes to the pastor doesn't count, five can become a burden, fifty change the situation. A pastor in a diocese doesn't count, five get noticed, fifty are unbeatable.

And So:

The officially established parish councils, priests' councils, pastoral councils, dioceses, and nations become a powerful instrument of renewal whenever individuals stand up decisively and unafraid for specific goals in their own domain and in the Church as a whole At the same time, however, the free groups of priests and laypeople are indispensable nowadays for helping certain causes in the Church to make a breakthrough. The organizations of priests and other forms of Catholic solidarity in various countries have achieved a great deal. They deserve increased support, in print as well. The cooperation of the different groups should not be disturbed by sectarian encapsulation, but must be strengthened for the sake of the common goal. In particular the contact of priests' groups with many nonfunctioning married priests must be maintained with a view toward their return to full churchly service.

Searching for Intermediate Solutions

Discussions alone do not help. Often one must show that one means business. Pressure on church authorities in the spirit of Christian fraternity can be legitimate where Christian office holders do not live up to their mandate. Use of the vernacular in every part of the Catholic liturgy, change in the regulations for mixed marriages, the affirmation of tolerance, democracy, human rights, and much else in church history was brought about only through continual pressure from below.

And So:

Wherever a measure taken by the superordinate church authority openly contradicts the gospel, resistance can be permitted and even required. Wherever an urgent measure on the part of church authorities is unacceptably delayed, provisional solutions may be set in motion in a prudent and balanced fashion, so long as church unity is maintained. To take a particularly difficult problem as an example: With the law of celibacy, because it is anchored in canon law and has legal sanctions behind it, any change against the will of the Church's leadership is almost impossible. A priest who after mature deliberation intends to marry should no longer secretly withdraw from his office but give his parish timely notice of it. If the community wishes him to stay, it will use every means to prevent the priest in question from leaving. Whatever rights a layman or married deacon has (the liturgy of the Word, preaching, baptizing, instruction, group work, etc.) can scarcely be denied a married priest, even if the law of celibacy is maintained. Until the matter is regulated for the whole Church it would be advisable for the sake of church unity that this priest abstain from presiding over the Eucharist. But if we can actively work to solve the question of celibacy — as with the question of the election of bishops, which is legally just as difficult and likewise increasingly urgent — then a fortiori we can do so on other issues, some of which are much more important, where legal sanctions are not at stake: the shaping of preaching and religious instruction, the liturgy and ecumenical cooperation, the protection of minorities and the victims of discrimination.

Not Giving Up

As the Church is renewed the greatest temptation or often too the comfortable alibi is to say that nothing does any good, that no progress is being made, and one would do better to take off: internal or external emigration. Meantime, where hope is lacking, so is action.

And So:

Precisely in this phase of stagnation the crucial point is to hold out serenely in trusting faith and to maintain staying power. Resistance was to be expected. But there can be no renewal without a struggle. Thus it remains crucial not to lose sight of the goal, to act quietly and decisively and to maintain hope in a Church that is more obligated to the Christian message and hence more open, more humane, more credible, in brief more Christian.

Why is there reason for hope? Because the future of the Church has already begun, because the will to renewal is not limited to certain groups, because the new inner polarizations can be overcome, because many and, in fact, the best bishops and pastors, like the directors of religious communities, affirm and promote thoroughgoing change. But also because the Church cannot stop the development of the world and because too the history of the Church itself is going on. Finally and actually first of all because we have faith that the power of the gospel of Jesus Christ continually proves stronger than all human incapacity and superficiality, than our own laziness, folly, and resignation.

Postscript

This declaration was drawn up in Tübingen in 1972 on the basis of a sketch by the author and was signed by the following thirty-three theologians and distributed in several languages:

Jean-Paul Audet (Montreal)
Alfons Auer (Tübingen)
Gregory Baum (Toronto)
Günther Biemer (Freiburg)
Franz Böckle (Bonn)
Viktor Conzemius (Lucerne)
Leslie Dewart (Toronto)
Casiano Floristán (Madrid)
Norbert Greinacher (Tübingen)
Winfried Gruber (Graz)
Herbert Haag (Tübingen)
Frans Haarsma (Nijmegen)
Bas Van Iersel (Nijmegen)
Otto Karrer (Lucerne)
Walter Kasper (Tübingen)
Ferdinand Klostermann (Vienna)
Hans Küng (Tübingen)

Peter Lengsfeld (Münster)
Juan Llopis (Barcelona)
Norbert Lohfink (Frankfurt am Main)
Richard McBrien (Boston)
John L. McKenzie (Chicago)
Johann Baptist Metz (Münster)
Johannes Neumann (Tübingen)
Franz Nikolasch (Salzburg)
Stephan Pfürtner (Fribourg)
Edward Schillebeeckx (Nijmegen)
Piet Schoonenberg (Nijmegen)
Gerard S. Sloyan (Philadelphia)
Leonard Swidler (Philadelphia)
Evangelista Villanova (Montserrat)
Herman-Josef Vogt (Tübingen)
Bonifac Willems (Nijmegen)

18

The Cologne Declaration
"Against Disenfranchism:
For an Open Catholicity"
(1989)

A number of events in our Catholic Church compel us to make the following public declaration.

We are deeply distressed by difficulties in three specific areas:

1. The Roman curia is aggressively pursuing a strategy of unilaterally filling vacant episcopal sees around the world, without regard for the recommendations of the local church and without respect for their established rights.

2. All over the world, many qualified theologians, men and women, are being denied ecclesiastical permission to teach. This represents a serious and dangerous interference in the free exercise of scholarly research and teaching, and in the pursuit of theological understanding through dialogue, principles which Vatican II repeatedly emphasized. The power to withhold official permission to teach is being abused; it has become an instrument to discipline theologians.

3. There have been theologically questionable attempts to assert the pope's doctrinal and jurisdictional authority in an exaggerated form.

What we observe seems to indicate the following changes in the postconciliar Church: a creeping extension of exaggerated hierarchical control; progressive undermining of the local churches, suppression of theological debate, and reduction in the role of the laity in the Church; antagonism from above which heightens conflict in the Church through means of disciplinary measures.

Because of our responsibility for the Christian faith; as an exercise of our ministry as teachers of theology; for the sake of our own consciences; and in solidarity with all Christian women and men who are scandalized by the latest developments in our Church, or even despair of it, we cannot remain silent but consider this declaration a necessity.

1. *In view of Rome's recent episcopal appointments around the world, but especially in Austria, Switzerland, and here in Cologne, we declare:*
Local churches have traditional, even codified canonical rights, to share in decision-making. Until today these rights have been part of the Church's history; they are part of its multilayered life.

The disciplining of local churches by episcopal appointments or by other measures (as in Latin America, Sri Lanka, Spain, the Netherlands, Austria, Switzerland, and here in Cologne) is often based on false analyses and suspicions. Such disciplinary actions rob the local churches of their autonomy. One of the critical achievements of Vatican II — the opening of the Catholic Church to collegiality between pope and bishops — is being stifled by recent Roman efforts at centralization.

The autocratic methods manifest in recent episcopal appointments stand in contradiction to the gospel spirit of brotherhood, to the positive, postconciliar experiences of freedom, and to the collegiality of the bishops.

This tendency hinders the ecumenical movement in essential ways.

With regard to "The Cologne Affair," we consider it scandalous that the election procedure was altered while the process was already underway. The sense of procedural justice is palpably offended.

Respect for and the dignity of the papal office require that power be exercised in a judicious manner in dealing with established institutions. The selection of candidates for the office of bishop should give proportionate recognition to all levels of the Church; the appointment process is not a private decision of the pope.

In today's world, the role of the nuncios becomes more and more questionable. While the means for sending news and for conducting personal consultations have been improved, the nunciature increasingly falls under the odium of being an intelligence agency, which through its one-sided selection of information is often responsible for creating the very deviations it is supposed to be looking for.

The kind of obedience toward the pope that recently and increasingly often has been demanded of bishops and cardinals, and affirmed by them, appears to be blind obedience. Ecclesial obedience in service of the gospel requires a readiness for constructive opposition (see the Code of Canon Law, 212, 3). We call on the bishops to remember the example of Paul, who remained in communion with Peter, even though on the question of the mission to the Gentiles, he "opposed him to his face" (Gal. 2:11).

2. With respect to the problem of appointing theology professors and granting ecclesiastical permission to teach, we declare:

The authority and responsibility of the local bishop to grant or to withhold ecclesiastical permission to teach must be preserved: this has a theological basis and to some extent is also guaranteed by concordats. The bishops are not executive agents of the pope. The current practice of violating the principle of subsidiarity in the Church in instances where the local bishop clearly has authority in questions of faith and morals is indefensible. Roman intervention in granting or denying permission to teach without consulting the local church or even acting against the explicit judgment of the local bishop risks undermining established and approved areas of juridical procedure.

Objections against authorizing someone to teach, or final decisions in these matters, must rest on legitimate reasons and be substantiated in accordance with recognized academic norms. Arbitrariness in this area puts the continued existence of Catholic theological faculties at state universities at risk.

The teachings of the Church are not all equally certain or of equal theological weight; there are degrees of theological certitude and a "hierarchy of truths." We object to the disregard shown this principle in the current practice of granting or denying ecclesiastical permission to teach. Individual matters of detail in ethical and dogmatic propositions cannot be arbitrarily exaggerated and raised to the point that they become the means of testing or questioning the integrity of a person's faith, while at the same time ethical positions directly connected to the practice of the faith (such as the rejection of torture, racial segregation, or exploitation) do not seem to hold the same theological importance for the integrity of the faith.

The right of universities or faculties to add to their numbers by selecting professors may not be completely eroded by arbitrary procedures in granting or denying ecclesiastical permission to teach. If under such pressures, the selection of university theology professors, female and male, takes place on the basis of criteria having nothing to do with the science of theology itself, then theology will suffer a loss of respect in the universities.

3. As for the attempt to assert the teaching authority of the pope in an unacceptable way, we declare:

Recently in addresses to theologians and bishops, and without considering the differing degrees of certitude and the unequal weight of church statements, the pope has connected the teaching on birth control with fundamental truths of the faith, such as the holiness of God and salvation through Jesus Christ. As a result, critics of the papal teaching on birth control find themselves condemned for "attacking fundamental cornerstones of Christian doctrine." Indeed, their very appeal to the dignity of an erroneous conscience is condemned. And they are accused of making "the cross of Christ of no avail," of "destroying the mystery of God," and denying the dignity of the human person. The pope draws upon the concepts of "fundamental truth" and "divine revelation" in order to defend a highly particular teaching, which can be grounded neither in Holy Scripture nor in the traditions of the Church (see his addresses of October 15 and November 12, 1988).

The interconnectedness of truths which the pope maintains does not mean that these truths are all of the same rank or the same importance. This is what Vatican II teaches: "In comparing doctrines with one another it should not be forgotten that there is an order of precedence or 'hierarchy' of truths within Catholic doctrine, according to the different ways they are connected with the foundation of Christian faith" (Decree on Ecumenism, 11). Similarly, the various degrees of certitude that may be attributed to theological statements and the limits of theological knowledge in medical and anthropological questions must be taken into account.

Even the papal teaching office has acknowledged the importance of theology itself for examining the arguments for theological statements and norms. This value may not be undermined by forbidding people to think and speak. Scientific investigation requires argumentation and communication. Conscience is not an executive assistant to the papal teaching office, as it might appear in the aforementioned addresses. It is much more the case that in arriving at its interpretation of the truth, the teaching office is dependent on the conscience of the faithful. To simply gloss over the tension between teaching and conscience leads in the end to a devaluation of conscience.

Many people in the Church are convinced that the norms for birth control in the encyclical *Humanae vitae* (1968) represent a moral position that does not replace the responsibility of the faithful to their own conscience. Bishops, among others the German bishops in their "Königstein Declaration" (1968), and moral theologians have considered this interpretation of many Christian women and men correct because they are convinced that the dignity of the conscience consists not only in obedience but also and precisely in responsibility. A pope who refers so often to the responsibility of Christian women and men in secular activities should not systematically disregard it in this critical area. Moreover, we regret the intense fixation of the papal teaching office on this single problem area.

The Church stands in the service of Jesus Christ. It must resist the constant temptation to misuse his gospel message about God's justice, mercy, and fidelity for the sake of its own power by resorting to questionable ways of governing. The Church was understood by the council as the pilgrim people of God and the living community of the faithful (*communio*). The Church is not a city under siege that expands its fortifications and rigidly defends itself against enemies within and without.

On the basis of our common witness, we share these various concerns about the Church with the pastors of the Church. To come to the defense of poor churches, to lead rich churches out of their entanglements, and to promote the unity of the Church, these are goals that we understand and which we support.

Theologians, who stand in the service of the Church, nevertheless also have the obligation to voice public criticism if church authority uses its power falsely so that it ends in contradicting its own goals, endangers the path to church unity, and retreats from the openness of Vatican II.

The pope claims to exercise the office of unity. In cases of conflict, therefore, it is part of his office to bring people together. In this, he went to excessive lengths with regard to Marcel Lefebvre and his followers, in spite of Lefebvre's fundamental challenge to the teaching magisterium. It is not part of the papal office to sharpen conflicts of a secondary nature without any attempt at dialogue, to resolve such conflicts unilaterally and by official decree, and to turn them into grounds for exclusion. If the pope does what does not belong to his office, he cannot demand obedience in the name of Catholicism. Then he must expect contradiction.

19

A Call for Renewal
in the Catholic Church
(1990)

In 1990 we celebrate the twenty-fifth anniversary of the historic document of the Second Vatican Council, "The Church in the Modern World" (*Gaudium et Spes*). This document clearly turned the face of the Church outward and defined its agenda as service to the entire human community. It stressed the importance of the laity bringing Christian values to the dialogue on the pressing issues facing society. Today our world desperately requires discernment of moral values in order to face the complex issues posed by

- a threatened environment,
- growing poverty in a world of affluence,
- a plague of drug usage which is both illness and symptom of deep despair,
- scientific advancements propelling us face to face with life decisions without the ethical principles to guide them,
- the challenge of reconciling nations and groups within nations when the temptation to the use of violence to resolve conflict has the potential of destroying our planet.

"A Call for Renewal in the Catholic Church" was drafted by Call to Action, an independent membership organization of laity, religious, and clergy committed to education and action on the social teaching of the Catholic Church in the spirit of Vatican II and the U.S. Catholic Bishops' Call to Action Conference (Detroit, 1976).

The Church should be providing the inspiration, support, guidance, wisdom, and encouragement to the community of believers to enter the dialogue on these issues. Unfortunately, today's Church is crippled by its failure to address fundamental justice issues within its own institutional structures and so becomes a stumbling block to its own members as well as to the broader society. Therefore we appeal to the institutional Church to undertake reform and renewal of its structures and to all the people of God to give witness of the Spirit who lives within us and seek ways to serve the vision of God in our human society.

We see women experiencing oppression, violence, and inequality in our world. Yet Vatican II's "Church in the Modern World" expresses respect for the fundamental rights of every person, and asserts that "every type of discrimination is to be overcome and eradicated as contrary to God's intent."

We call upon the Church to incorporate women at all levels of ministry and decision-making.

We see many Catholics deprived of the Church's sacramental life because of the declining number of priests. In particular, we see Catholics denied regular access to the Eucharist, the center of our worship and spiritual life.

We call upon the Church to discard the medieval discipline of mandatory priestly celibacy, and to open the priesthood to women and married men, including resigned priests, so that the Eucharist may continue to be the center of the spiritual life of all Catholics.

We see very few instances where the people of God are allowed by church authorities to participate in decisions that affect their lives. Yet in 1970 Karol Wojtyla, now Pope John Paul II, wrote in his book *The Acting Person:* "Any authentic community is founded on participation. . . . [Its structure] is correct only if it admits the practical effectiveness of opposition required by the common good and the right of participation."

We call for continued extensive consultation with Catholic women and men in the development of church teaching in the area of social justice. We call for the same consultative process in developing church teaching on human sexuality.

We see the pope and the Roman curia selecting bishops throughout the world without input from local churches. Yet, as stated in the Cologne

Declaration of 1989 and supported by hundreds of theologians from many nations, "The procedure of nomination is not some private choice of the pope's."

We claim our responsibility, as committed laity, religious, and clergy, to participate in the selection of our local bishops, a time honored tradition in the Church.

We see groups marginalized in our Church because of race and ethnic identity.

We call for the Church to speed up the enculturation of diverse peoples through new forms of liturgy, language, and leadership drawn from the indigenous culture of the people.

We see theologians silenced, constructive opposition condemned, loyalty oaths imposed, and blind obedience demanded.

We call for open dialogue, academic freedom, and due process.

We see the Church conducting financial dealings in secret without accountability to her people.

We call upon the Church to become a model of financial openness on all levels, including the Vatican.

We see the Vatican downgrading the importance of national bishops conferences.

We affirm the collegial and collaborative leadership style of the U.S. Catholic Conference of Bishops and call upon the universal Church to affirm this traditional and effective exercise of church leadership.

We see the pain of countless people at the closing of their parishes and schools throughout the United States.

We call for a process that allows all those affected to be heard from, and to take part in these decisions.

We see many young adults and children of Catholic families who are reluctant to affiliate with a Church they view as authoritarian and hypocritical.

We call for a fundamental change so that young people will see and hear God living in and through the Church as a participatory community of believers who practice what they preach.

We call on all people within our Church, in the spirit of co-discipleship and co-responsibility, to use their imagination and creativity. Working together we can make the Church more faithful to her mission, proclaimed in "The Church in the Modern World," to be a sign of God's saving work and a servant to the human community.

Sources

1. "Why I Am Staying in the Church" originally appeared in *America*, March 20, 1971.

2. "Why I Remain a Catholic" originally appeared in *The Church Maintained in Truth* by Hans Küng, translated by Edward Quinn. Copyright © 1980 by The Seabury Press, Inc.

3. "Catholics and Protestants: An Ecumenical Inventory" originally appeared in *Signposts for the Future* by Hans Küng, translated by Edward Quinn. Translation copyright © 1978 by Doubleday, a division of Bantam, Doubleday, Dell Publishing Group, Inc. Used by permission of the publisher.

4. "Parties in the Church?," translated by Francis McDonagh, originally appeared in *Polarization in the Church, Concilium* 88, edited by H. Küng and W. Kasper. Copyright © 1973 by Herder and Stichting Concilium.

6. "Church from Above — Church from Below" was first published by the Catholic Renewal Movement, London, 1985.

8. "On the Way to a New Church Order: A Theological Case for Shared Decision-Making by the Laity," translated by Arlene Swidler, originally appeared under the title "Participation of the Laity in Church Leadership and in Church Elections" in *Journal of Ecumenical Studies* 6, no. 4 (Fall 1969). Reprinted with permission of the publisher.

9. "Free Election of Bishops: A Concrete Model," translated by John Maxwell, originally appeared in *Electing Our Own Bishops, Concilium* 137, edited by P. Huizing and K. Walf. New York: Seabury Press/ Edinburgh: T. & T. Clark, 1980.

10. "Women in Church and Society" originally appeared in *The New York Times Magazine*, May 23, 1976, under the title "Feminism: A New Reformation." Copyright © 1976 by The New York Times Company.

12. "Worship Today — Why?" originally appeared in *Signposts for the Future* by Hans Küng, translated by Edward Quinn. Translation copyright © 1978 by Doubleday, a division of Bantam, Doubleday, Dell Publishing Group, Inc. Used by permission of the publisher.

15. "My Personal *Spero* — The Vision of a Better Future" was translated by Arlene Swidler.

18. The Cologne Declaration, translated by Karen Trub, William Dych, S.J., and Leonard Swidler, is reprinted with permission from the February 14, 1989, issue of *Commonweal*.